DON'T GET
MAD
GET WISE

DON'T GET

MAD

GET WISE

DON'T GET
MAD
GET WISE

Why no one ever makes you angry... ever!

MIKE GEORGE

PENTAGON PRESS

Don't get MAD get wise

ISBN 10: 81-8274-279-X
ISBN 13: 978-81-8274-279-6

First Indian Edition 2007

Original English Edition published by O Books, (imprint of John Hunt Publishing Ltd.) UK. Indian Edition published in arrangement by Pentagon Press

First Published in India by

Pentagon Press
A-38 Hauz Khas
New Delhi-110016
Ph. +91-11-41517091, 41656996, 7, 8
Fax: +91-11-41656997
Email: pentagonpress@airtelbroadband.in

Printed at Brijbasi Art Press Ltd., Noida.

Dedication

*To those who lose the plot, see the red rag and allow that
mist to descend on a regular basis.*

*To those who intuitively know that peace is already and
always present within their heart, but cannot 'get at it'.*

*To those who wish to forgive so they may free themselves
of the burden of their hurts.*

If you have any questions or comments regarding any
of the ideas/insights in this book, please talk to me at
mike@relax7.com

For further insights, visualisations and meditations
visit www.relax7.com

Contents

3 **Why Forgiveness Always Heals**
     The Wisdom and the Way

Introduction

We all know anger. We also know how it kills our inner peace. And while most of us like the idea of forgiveness, it often seems a difficult thing to practise, especially when the source of our hurt is up close and personal.

Perhaps never before in the history of this world has there been so much anger, resentment and peacelessness in the hearts and minds of men and women. We are saturated with stories of rage, terror and revenge by the news media. The entertainment industries bring us a continuous stream of crafted tales of insult, indignation and resentment. Anger is almost an industry in its own right. Meanwhile, just outside our own homes there are increasing levels of neighbourly noise, more devious builders, cheating partners and yobbish behaviours undermining the fabric of our communities. All apparently good reasons to be grumpy, if not incensed.

But that's the big picture, and big pictures are not that important until the little picture is clear. The little picture is YOU and your feelings. How angry are you? Do you ever get angry? Does your temperament simmer with a quiet resentment...occasionally? Be honest. To say everyone gets angry every day sounds like a big general claim that is impossible to prove because it is impossible to know. However, I suspect it's true. Is it true for you?

This book is a response to a call, that is both conscious and unconscious, for understanding and release from the pain that is anger. I hear this call every day, especially in the work I do, a large part of which is teaching, training and coaching in organisations. In many ways I do not feel qualified to respond because there are so many 'experts' out there. Yet, in other ways, I not only feel highly qualified, I feel compelled to write this book after nearly 25 years studying anger and its many forms both within myself and in the lives of others.

I have not studied in an academic, psychological or therapeutic sense, though I have looked over the shoulders of some who have, and I do understand their views and their techniques. The study that produces this three-part reflection is spiritually based. It comes from a personal passion for truth. For the last two and a half decades I've been lucky to be able to devote huge amounts of time and energy to exploring what is true and what is false about anger and forgiveness.

It is out of the intensity of these years that this book comes. It is from the ultimate simplicity of what I would call the 'spiritual point of view' (see page 11) that I attempt to keep these reflections and insights into anger, peace and forgiveness as simple and essenceful as possible. Sometimes simple seems too simple, essence too essenceful, especially if our tendency is to want lots of explanation, backed up by precise detail. But that tendency is too often the way of avoiding the truth, which is always simple, which always returns to the essence of things. If it doesn't, be suspicious! The truth about anger is therefore quite simple and its remedy also quite simple, in theory at least.

The truth also acts as a mirror. It reflects and exposes the illusions and the falsehoods that have become engraved within our thought patterns and our personality over time. When we see these illusions, and feel our own lack of authenticity, we may feel uncomfortable to the point of resistance, and perhaps further into irritation. It means that even while we are searching for answers to our mental and emotional discomforts, we don't want to see too deeply into their causes, because it means we will have to change. We have become comfortable being uncomfortable, happy being unhappy, perversely content with our anger. In that moment we forget why we are searching, why we are reading in the first place, which is to find the wisdom and the ways that can help us free ourselves from our mental and emotional discomfort, and restore true peace to our heart.

I hope you find the insights in these pages the kind that trigger your discomfort and resistance. They would have less value to you if they didn't. I hope they may also help you to realise that you can change your beliefs and your perceptions and, as a consequence, your attitudes and behaviours in particular, and then your life in general. The paradox at the heart of the plethora of self help, spiritual wisdom and so called life changing philosophies is that when you do encounter what is true, you are only reminding your self of what you already know.

It may seem like the book, the seminar, the guru is giving you all the answers, but they don't. You do. You already know, you only forgot. This book serves only to remind.

Finally, if you like a bit of anger you probably won't like this book, if you use anger to motivate others you will probably pooh-pooh this book, and if you are the kind who is always judging and criticising others then you'll probably throw this book at the wall in disgust when you realise you have been wasting your time and energy. So that about covers us all I guess!

As always, I'm available for any comments and questions at mike@relax7.com

From the 'Spiritual Point of View'

Every situation and event can be viewed from different angles. Everyone creates a different perspective of the same events and circumstances. Perception is personal. How you perceive and interpret the world is influenced by your learned beliefs, past experiences and most of all your sense of identity. The same applies as you view what appears to happen within your self. Some people seek to explain thinking patterns, feelings and emotions from a purely psychological point of view, where psyche is often simply an aspect of brain chemistry, a function of our physical body. However I prefer to see, to perceive, from the deepest perspective.

I prefer to reach beyond the psyche and the psychological to perceive and understand inner events such as beliefs, thoughts and emotions from the spiritual point of view. That means I view through the understanding that spirit/soul is what you are, what I am. That means I am/you are not the body I/you occupy and animate. We are certainly not our brains, they are, in words of Robin Williams' angel in the film *Dreams May Come*, just 'pieces of meat'! I am/you are the energy that is non-physical, self-aware, indestructible and invisible, located within the body just above and behind the eyes. Soul/self/spirit/consciousness are basically synonymous with 'me', with 'you'! It is the 'I' that says I AM. When the body decays and falls apart the soul/self does not.

While none of this can be proved scientifically, this realisation of true self can generate many real and profound shifts in your understanding of your self. Perhaps the two most relevant, as we begin our journey into anger, are first, you are totally responsible for everything you think and feel and do at all times in all situations. Second, you cannot die. Both are quite radical insights in a world that teaches us to believe and live the opposite. Both have the power to change your life when realised and integrated into your life.

If this does not sit easily with your current belief system, I ask you to suspend your beliefs during the time it takes you to read this book. For me, to see and understand anger from a spiritual viewpoint, to understand the concept of forgiveness with 'spiritual awareness' is the only way to reveal the absolute truth about anger and forgiveness.

I don't write to convince you of anything, to prove a point or to make a case. I write primarily to set down as clearly and simply as possible the truth as 'I see it now' and, in the process, offer some insights which may be of value in your day-to-day life. Please do not believe a word I say! Use the words, ideas, reflections and insights as signposts that can direct you towards where and how to look for your self, so that you can 'see for your self' and realise what is true for you. That will require some form of reflective or meditative practice, which I describe in part 2. If you have no understanding of anything 'spiritual' whatsoever, be prepared for your 'spiritual eye' to open. If you are way down the other end of the scale and think you are very spiritual, prepare to have your eye recalibrated and refocused!

Many have learned to believe that they are not only spiritual but divinity itself, that God is omnipresent and therefore 'in them'. Take a moment to reflect and you may see that if you were a being in a divine (God like) state right now, or if God were present within you right now (omnipresence), you would not be ignorant of anything, you would never search for anything, you would never be impressed by anything or anyone, you would never crave or be averse to anyone or anything, and anger would be an almost laughable impossibility. And most certainly you would not be reading this book!

I have come to suspect that when we believe that God is everywhere, in everything and in everyone, or that everything and everyone is in God, it is a sign of a 'lazy spirituality'. It can provide a convenient excuse to not make the effort to have a direct, dynamic and very personal relationship with God. If we believe God is within and that God gets angry, it is easier to therefore justify our own anger. It can suppress the humility that we need to be a student of truth, and it delays the awakening of our true awareness of who and what we are as individual and unique beings. Now, more than ever before we need to not just know who we are, but learn to 'be who we are', if we are to transform emotions such as anger, to which we become easily addicted.

In my humble opinion, the spiritual point of viewing anything can begin only when you correct the 'great mistake' and realise your self as spirit and not form, when you realise that what you see in the mirror is not you, when you realise that the material world outside you cannot be owned, controlled or ever make you, the spiritual being, content.

'Spiritual' is one of those words that is increasingly attracting many different meanings, many varied perceptions, depending on learned beliefs and experiences. Like 'love', is fast becoming a word that is wrongly used and abused. If you would like to explore further what it 'spiritual' means please look at www.SpiritualIntelligenceUnit.com.

I will make occasional reference to the spiritual point of view throughout, so I hope this may clarify what I mean when I do. If not, please send me your questions by email. It's important.

Cards on the Table

As you make your way through the three main sections, you'll notice that I don't call on academic authority or on today's therapeutic specialists. I also avoid the more ancient authorities of the various religious or philosophical scriptures. I do this because I recognise you as the real authority in your own life. Dependency on the beliefs of others, however attractively expressed, can make you lazy. You have the capacity to fully understand and transform your anger, rediscover the power of your own peace and realise for your self the true way of forgiveness.

There are no techniques and no tools that can replace the power of realisation to transform the essential 'self' and free you from the illusions, delusions and confusions which keep you stuck in old patterns and habits of self-created suffering. We are all emotionally suffering now, even though we may not be aware of it, even though we may have renamed our suffering as 'necessary', even good, as many have!

By all means practise breathing techniques, relaxation exercises and even the most recently publicised emotional freedom techniques which involve tapping the meridians that run through your body. They can all bring relief to the symptoms of emotional discomfort, but none can deliver a lasting cure. That requires a process of seeing, feeling, knowing and being the truth, being your true self. That takes time, regular introspection and the patient practice of meditation, which is not so much a technique as a deepening of self-awareness.

Part One sets out what I have come to see and understand as the real causes and consequences of anger.

It's probably best to declare my hand from the outset. For me, anger kills, full stop. If it doesn't kill your body, it murders your capacity to be creative. And that's the very purpose of your life, to be creative. Anger is never healthy, never positive and never justified. Many books, seminars, philosophers and so-called experts on the human personality have argued that anger is a natural, biological and psychological response which fits neatly into human survival and the evolution of the species. While I accept that as a point of view, while I can understand why some have that belief, I don't agree with any of them. From a spiritual point of view, which means a view based on what is absolutely true, anger is never ever healthy, natural or useful. I used to be very angry, I used to get very angry and I used to celebrate the anger of others. But after some time I realised it was draining and counter-productive. I realised that anger is the enemy of the peaceful, contented and fulfilling life. It totally destroys the ability to create meaningful relationships and consistently good work. If you are a believer in the necessity of anger, I ask you only to stop and reflect deeply and see if you can see how it is a huge obstacle to your own contentment and fulfilment, and how it influences the contentment and fulfilment of those around you. Keep an open mind. Let me know if I am not being clear.

Part Two is an exploration into the nature of peace and peace as our nature.

Just as the poison of a snakebite has an antidote, so too the venom of anger has an antidote, which is a combination of truth and peace. These are the two things, the two inner conditions, that never ever leave you. Both abide eternally within each one of us. You already know the truth about anger and you can invoke your inner peace at will. It's just that you lose awareness of what is true and forget the practice of calm. Anger is a sign that you have lost awareness of the truth of 'who I am', and that something is blocking your access to the peace of your heart. Not your physical heart but your spiritual heart. Peace is also married to love and you may have noticed that it is impossible to feel loving and angry at the same time. In fact it is love that heals your spiritual heart, that you your self have wounded by your anger-driven habits over time. While most of us search for love and peace from the hearts of others, it means we have not yet realised that we already have what we seek within our own hearts. To heal the scars of anger, which can range from violent rages to simmering resentment, it is essential to rediscover the truth of who are and the peace of what you are.

Part Three focuses on forgiveness and the other most common responses to any sense of personal hurt.

You'll need to be sitting comfortably with a very open mind for this, as it ultimately reveals the deepest truth about anger, why no one ever makes you angry and the idea that YOU have never been angry! Most cultures acknowledge forgiveness as a good thing to do. Most religions encourage its practice. But the deepest truth about forgiveness is that you never need to do it because you have never been wronged. To believe you have been hurt is mostly an illusion. Paradoxically however, in order to break free of the grip of the illusion that you have been wronged and hurt by another, and to realise the truth that you haven't, you will need to forgive your way there. In order to forgive your way to freedom from all hurt, you will need to understand and accept the utter futility of the anger itself, and then recognise the irrelevance of the learned 'forgiveness response' towards those whom you mistakenly believed made you angry.

Take a Moment to Reflect

Before you begin the journey through this book it helps to take a moment to reflect on your current awareness of its main themes (anger/peace/forgiveness) in your life. As you reflect, it will help you to recognise, grasp and apply the insights that you may discover here with greater ease and effectiveness.

1 What is anger for you?

2 How would you describe the most common form
 of anger that you experience within yourself

3 What sets off your anger most?

4 Is anger of any use and if so how could you use it?

5 What does peace mean to you?

6 When are you at your most peaceful

7 How do you think you can create peace in your life?

8 Why do you think the experience of inner peace
 is so elusive for many people?

9 What is forgiveness?

10 Why do you think it is so difficult to forgive?

1 | **Why Anger always Destroys**
The Pain and the Problem

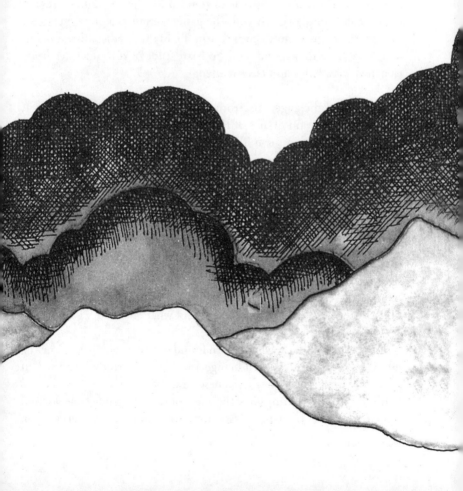

The Red Mist

It's the third round of the men's singles during the annual festival of smash and volley at Wimbledon. Greg Rusedski is one set up and cruising to victory. At a crucial moment half way though the second set, a member of the crowd calls a ball out. The umpire thinks it's a line judge, so he accepts the call and Rusedski goes berserk. The British number two loses the point and the plot. The red mist descends and the nation hears a series of expletives directed at the umpire. Rackets are smashed as he falls apart and loses the match. In the interview that follows he honestly admits his opponent did not win the match as much as his anger lost it. It is a classic example of how anger, sometimes referred to as the 'incendiary emotion', destroys concentration and kills performance. And yet, when the exact same series of events happens to the Federers and the Agassis of this world, they are almost totally unfazed and simply get on with the game. Tennis is a great metaphor for life. Both are a game, both feature highly unpredictable events to which we have to respond, and both are a lot of fun, until teeth are clenched, eyes bulge and faces redden.

At one end of the anger spectrum are those who get angry quickly at the sight or mention of any of hundreds of apparent injustices in the world. Somewhere in the middle are those who generally remain calm with the 'big stuff' that happens far away in the world, but who are easily irritated by the 'small stuff' which happens within relationships and events closer to home. At the other end of the spectrum there are some who would call themselves enlightened, and for whom anger in any shape or form is no more. They would say that anger serves no purpose and is counter-productive. Then there's the angry activist who says that the world will not change for the better without someone getting upset with the way things are. So who is right? Does anger have a place in creating a better world? Can anger ever be healthy? Is it ever justified? What is anger? Why does it happen? And what effect does it have?

In numerous studies, anger has been found to have a wholly detrimental effect on our physical well-being. In one such study, reported at a recent conference on forgiveness and peace in the US, it was demonstrated that letting go of the anger buried in a grudge relieved and reduced chronic back pain. Another study discovered that women fighting their own substance abuse were able to reduce the length of relapses by practising forgiveness. The Standford University forgiveness project revealed how it is impossible to be happy and healthy while carrying bitterness and anger at how unjustly we might have been treated.

It seems we have been conditioned to treat any tension-triggering event, be it a police siren or a simmering conflict with a partner or colleague, as a crisis. At these moments our bodies generate and release the stress hormones adrenaline and cortisol. Our heart accelerates, our breath quickens and our mind races. The release of sugar that accompanies our reaction revs up the muscles and our blood surges with increased clotting factors. It's all harmless if the tension or fright is brief and very infrequent, like a near miss while driving, but the emotional disturbances of anger and resentment are like accidents that don't end, and hormones turn into toxins. The depressive effect of cortisol upon the immune system has been linked to serious diseases and disorders. According to Professor Stafford Lightman of Bristol University, "Cortisol wears down the brain, leading to cell atrophy and memory loss. It also raises blood pressure and blood sugar, hardening the arteries, leading to heart disease." Anger does not get good press among the medical fraternity.

You cannot be serious!

Yes it's true; one of the greatest tennis players was an angry young man for most of his career. John McEnroe seemed to be able to turn anger into successful performance. Three factors are worth considering here. One is how his anger storms were like flares, and how he was able to switch them on and off so quickly that they did not affect his concentration... so much. Second, he had such an abundance of natural talent and what appeared to be an unlimited supply of determination, it more than outweighed his loss of emotional control. Third, how many more trophies and tournaments would he have won if his natural talent had not been sabotaged by his angry outbursts?

It's Not Them – It's You!

Take a moment to reflect on the last time you became angry at someone. It can be hard to see that your anger is never created by anyone other than your self. Though it 'seems' the other person's actions are responsible for your emotional state, in truth it is simply your 'response' to the person or the event. Every response you create can be a conscious choice. You simply forget that you have a choice and that you do not have to react angrily. This choice is easily obscured as the anger seems to arise within you naturally, and you probably even believe it is instinctive, and therefore something that is healthy and that you need do nothing about. Which is why many people argue for their anger and become easily irritated in any conversation with someone who disagrees!

Anger usually means you are running on autopilot, allowing your subconscious habits of belief and perception to shape your nearly conscious thoughts and actions. The mental action of creating anger itself becomes a habit. It also displays a mental and emotional laziness, and when it happens you have less intelligence than a robot. It's impossible to think clearly and make accurate decisions when you are angry. In order to free your self from the anger habit you will need to take three significant steps:

- understand why anger is extremely unhealthy.
- accept responsibility for your anger, in whatever form it takes, at all times and in all situations.
- be prepared to expose, challenge and change the beliefs and perceptions you hold, which are creating your emotional pain.

In no way is anger wrong or bad, it simply has its roots in a set of false beliefs, and it emerges through learned and habitual patterns of behaviour. It is however, extremely unhealthy. If you start to believe in 'wrong' and 'bad' then you will likely suppress and repress your anger, and eventually your physical health will deteriorate and someone some day will be on the end of a volcanic outburst. Anger is simply a sign that you, not the object of your anger, have made a mistake. To see the mistake you need to raise your level of self-awareness. The purpose of this book is to help you see within your self what you have not yet seen, a belief or a perception that you hold that is misleading you. And then drop it.

As you raise your self-awareness, you will also see how your anger begins with a moment of irritation towards a person or situation. If you then give attention to that irritation by replaying the event in your mind, which is like giving water to a plant, it will grow into frustration. And if you water the frustration, it will grow into anger, which, in turn, will develop into rage.

Anger is learned and it can therefore be unlearned. That means don't repress, don't suppress and don't express. What's left? Transform. The transformation of anger requires insight into the root cause of your emotional pain. When you see the cause it gives you a choice a) to stop creating it or b) continue creating it. Unfortunately, although many see why they cause their own anger and acknowledge responsibility for their creation, they continue to do so. They find many ways of justifying their anger. They have an 'anger addiction'. They are angerholics.

Are you ready to see the root cause? Do you want to make new choices? Is it time to break your emotional addiction? Yes? Then read on. No? Then you can resell this book at Amazon now!

When change equals choice

In a world where our education seeks to prepare us for the 'production/ consumption' society we learn how to make choices at the supermarket and in the holiday brochures. Unfortunately we receive no education regarding how to choose and change our beliefs and our feelings. No one shows us how our thoughts and feelings are rooted in our beliefs and that there are more enlightened choices that can transform our life and therefore our destiny. Awareness leads to seeing, which leads to understanding, which leads to expansion of choice. And that leads to the self-created opportunity to change.

Blinded by Fatal Beliefs

Irritation, frustration and full-blown anger are not pleasurable creations but moments of pain and suffering at a mental/emotional level. We are in fact inflicting that pain on ourselves (as we are always the creators of our own emotions), which could be likened to sticking a knife in your body. Would you choose to self inflict suffering? Most of us would not, but we don't realise what we are doing. So why do we do it? Why do YOU do it? There are seven fatal beliefs that we all tend to assimilate (learn) and use to justify and sustain our anger. Score each belief out of ten as they apply to you. 1 is low (no, I have never believed that) and 10 is high (yes, I have always believed that). Remember that most of your beliefs are now held in your subconscious, so it may take you a few moments of reflection to lower the line between conscious and subconscious and see what you actually believe. On a moment-to-moment, day-to-day basis your beliefs are revealed to your self by what you hear your self thinking and saying.

Remember, belief is not the truth. When you know the truth you don't need to believe anything, because you know! In each case I have identified the truth, which you already know but have just forgotten or not yet realised. Dwell on each truth and allow it to reawaken within your consciousness. In time it will give you the power to change.

Fatal Belief ONE
It's not me. It's them!

It only takes a moment of reflection to see how others are not responsible for your thoughts and feelings. At all times, and in all places, you and only you are the creator of your thoughts and feelings. To believe otherwise is to project the illusion that others are responsible for what you think and feel and to live a painful life filled with the continuous blaming of others.

Truth: You and only you are 100% responsible for what you think and feel at all times.

Transformational Tip: Stop watching the soaps on television or any scripted drama. If you do watch, see how the characters attempt to manipulate each other's emotions and how each episode is an attempt to manipulate your emotional state. See how easily you fall under the illusion that other people make you feel what you feel.

Fatal Belief TWO

I have no choice but to get angry

You believe you do not have a choice over your thoughts and feelings. No one ever taught you how to understand, manage and choose your feelings, especially when something happens that you do not like. "But what did you expect?" you say indignantly. "Of course I am going to get angry when you do that!"

Truth: Choice begins with your beliefs and perceptions. Self-transformation begins with increasing your awareness of the beliefs that you hold and that hold you!

Transformational Tip: Learn a method to increase self-awareness, like meditation or reflective enquiry. You will then see your choices much more clearly.

Fatal Belief THREE

It's quite normal to be angry

After many years of reinforcing learned behaviour patterns based on anger, you are in a kind of comfort zone. You have become comfortable with your emotional discomfort, which you then defend and justify by saying you believe it is 'normal' behaviour. You probably even think to yourself, "Everyone else is doing it so it must be OK."

Truth: Anger is totally abnormal for a sane human being. As we will see later, any moment of anger means you are temporarily insane.

Transformational Tip: Try becoming angry at the receipt of good news and you will begin to see how silly anger is. In fact you will begin to laugh.

Fatal Belief FOUR

It gives me energy

When you become angry it can seem to give you a surge of energy. The illusion is complete when you think it is positive energy. It is simply an emotional explosion within your consciousness that spills into your body and out into your behaviour. This surge of energy temporarily heightens your attention and alertness. Your body tenses and the fuse is about to blow. The outcome following a bout of anger is mental and emotional exhaustion. The anger actually drains your energy. Like a power surge on the national grid, the power stations are drained. Like water disappearing down the plughole of an emptying bath, the anger drains your power. However it is the 'hit' of adrenaline in your body that you become addicted to. Adrenaline is a physical stimulant and sometimes you may find yourself saying, "I only did it for the buzz"! This also reinforces the belief that a bit of anger is good.

Truth: Anger drains your energy and over time will end in burnout.

Transformational Tip: Every time you become angry visualise a white sail on a calm sea and a gentle, cool breeze blowing against your face.

Fatal Belief FIVE
It's a natural response to become angry
To close down your anger factory means you would need to detoxify your emotional and physical systems, and change the habit of a lifetime. That sounds like hard work, therefore the fifth belief, which you have willingly learned, is that anger is a 'natural' response, a healthy response, to other people's behaviour. You don't realise the danger it presents to your personal health and well-being. Maintaining the belief that anger is natural is also a way of avoiding the danger of being labelled 'unnatural' if you ever do decide to change. We collude to maintain the illusion that anger is OK, thus avoiding the inner work of changing a deep habit. This is also known as emotional laziness. The entertainment industry is right behind us on this one! Much fictional drama is designed to induce anger in different forms in order to hold our attention. Even the non-fictional drama known as 'the news' is packaged and represented in sensational ways that are subtly designed to trigger moral outrage.

Truth: Anger is a sure sign you are going against the grain of your true nature, which is peaceful and loving.

Transformational Tip: Watch the news with the sound down and practise staying peaceful and benevolent towards what and who you see, no matter what they appear to have done.

Fatal Belief SIX

I need to use anger to motivate others

This is so often the lament of many modern managers as they attempt quick motivational short cuts. They use anger to display their displeasure, knowing it will spark someone into acting differently. In truth however, it is never a good idea. Other people soon become resentful and eventually switch off, or simply avoid contact altogether. Trust and respect, the foundations of any relationship, most especially in the workplace, are never built by anger. In the long term, angry outbursts only demonstrate an absence of self-control, self-respect and laziness in relationships, all of which sabotage any leadership qualities they may have.

Truth: Anger kills motivation within oneself and will likely adversely influence others' motivation.

Transformational Tip: Consciously practice acceptance of others as they are and respect for others regardless of what they do (people are not what they do).

Fatal Belief SEVEN

You need to 'snarl' to survive

This is the belief that lies behind most wars, and millions suffer as a result. When we believe anger is essential to assertiveness, we will see signs of total confusion and the demise of civilisation. Anger is the opposite of assertiveness. When you snarl, you are killing yourself first and foremost, and those on the receiving end are only going to give back as good as they get, or run away completely. Anger weakens and diminishes the mental strength you need to get through difficult situations and unexpected events. Snarling kills the snarler from inside out, and often the snarled at, from outside in.

Truth: To make a real and lasting peace with others we need to be anger-free.

Most people are carriers of all seven of the above beliefs, but if just one is living within your belief system you will see no reason to stop being angry and you will continue to avoid the truth that you are harming your self first and foremost. Every year tens of thousands of young people receive hospital treatment for physical self-harm. Little do we realise that 'emotional self-harm' is happening every day in the lives of millions. It's called anger, and its effects can be seen in almost all other areas of our health service. We just don't make the connection between the most common mental disease and the many physical diseases that it triggers and sustains. Whenever you become angry you are emotionally self-harming.

A little anger in Japan!

For some time therapists have believed that anger is OK – in fact, many therapists still believe that it's good to get angry once in a while. Around fifteen years ago in Japan it was discovered that around 10,000 executives were dying every year from overwork (Karoshi) and they traced the cause to excessive, but suppressed, anger. So they created 'anger rooms' in the basements of their office blocks, padded the walls and put a baseball bat in the room. They told executives that if they felt anger coming on they should go to the room and just hit the walls with the bat as hard, and as much, as they wanted in order to get the anger out of their system. Two years later they measured the results. The amount of anger had increased. Why? After much head scratching they eventually realised that people who were going to the rooms regularly were practising getting angry and simply reinforcing the habit. The message – don't suppress, don't repress and don't express – transform.

The Wars in Your World

So why do you get angry? Only when you cultivate self-awareness through self-reflection are you able to see exactly where and why you create your anger. It always begins with a disturbance within your consciousness and it is always because the world around you is not dancing to your tune. Whenever you become angry, it is because you have an image in your mind of how things should be, how people should behave, how events should unfold, and the external reality is not matching the image in your mind. Anger comes when you are not inwardly flexible enough to accept that outward reality is always going to be different from your preconceptions, expectations and desires. In fact, your anger is a sign that you are trying and failing to control other people and events. You have not yet realised that you cannot control other people and events. The world is not designed to waltz to the sound of your swing band. This is why anger is often referred to as a moment of insanity. You are clinically insane! Why? Three reasons. You are out of control – the emotion is controlling you. You are totally irrational as the emotion kills your ability to think in a reasoned way. And you are trying (and of course failing) to do the impossible, which is to change what you cannot change - the past and other people. Images of babies, prams and flying toys spring to mind at this point!

"Since war begins in the minds of men..." is an accepted insight that is often quoted from the introduction of the Constitution of UNESCO. It is not the gun that kills, but the emotion that pulls the trigger. Anger is the killer. Any time you sense irritation, frustration or anger coming, be aware, and you will notice you are waging war on one of three fronts; with the past, with another person or with yourself.

You are at *war with the past* because your anger is always towards something that has already happened and your emotional reaction means you are trying to change it. Which is impossible. To the rest of the world it looks as if you believe you can. That's because you hold this belief subconsciously. Somewhere and sometime in the past, you have picked up and assimilated the belief that the world, including all other people, should do exactly what you want them to, or what you think they should do.

You are at *war with another person* because they have done something which you judge to be wrong and your anger is an attempt to change them or inflict revenge. Perhaps you have not yet realised that it is impossible to control others and make them change. The habit of anger is so deep that this truth, which will eventually become self-evident, has not yet killed the root of your illusion that anger is good. Even the worst dictators do not control other people. People make their own decisions and control their own actions, always. Certainly they can be influenced, but they cannot be controlled. Nelson Mandela's 27 years of exile reminds us that while they controlled the location of his body they could do nothing with his state of mind. Hence his ability to walk away from such an experience, without even a whiff of a desire for revenge in his heart or his eyes. Notice how this one attribute alone, this ability to forgive, almost qualified him to be the de facto leader of the world. It's as if we intuitively acknowledge that the individual who has freed themselves from all anger and dissolved any thoughts of revenge has earned our respect and deepest admiration, as we pin the badge of greatness on them.

You are at *war with yourself* because you are failing to make the world dance to your tune, or you believe you have let yourself down. Have you ever sat in a restaurant waiting for your meal, only to discover forty minutes later, that your order was forgotten or lost? You get upset, but with whom? Perhaps the waiter at first, but then with yourself, for failing to ask after fifteen minutes. There are two failures here. First you failed to speak sooner. Second, you failed to control your emotions. Although you might not verbally admit that you failed, inside you know. And so you start to beat yourself up. The old thought/feeling pattern goes something like this: to fail is to lose, to lose is to be sad, to be sad is the precursor to being angry, as you look for an external cause of your sadness which, in this case, is initially the waiter, so you demonstrate to others your righteous anger towards the waiter. But deep inside you know it is your self that has made you sad. So you get angry with your self... twice... once for the forty-minute loss of your order (which could have been five minutes if only you had said something) and second, for the loss of control over your own emotions. But that's too much to bear after a while, so again you find someone else outside on whom to project your anger. You send them a package marked "I'm angry with you!" You seem to feel better as a result, but it's only temporary. Daft, isn't it!

Be aware the next time you become angry. Interrupt the pattern of your anger by asking yourself two simple questions: What am I trying to do? Answer: You are trying to control what you cannot control (past and people). Who is suffering first and most? Answer: Yourself! And if your anger is directed at yourself for your own seeming failure then repeat this short phrase, "There is no such thing as failure, only a different outcome from the one that I expected." And if you insist on staying angry then ask yourself the question, "How long is my anger going to last?" You'll be surprised how fast it disappears.

Always Complaining?

To complain, you must have a picture in your mind of something better than what you already have, but that you are not willing to risk creating. If you cannot imagine anything better, then you will not complain. Problem: You'd rather complain than risk doing what's necessary to produce the "something better." Solution: Stop complaining and start taking the actions that will produce what you want. Caution: If you use anger to motivate someone else in this process it's almost guaranteed that you will a) get anger in return b) induce defensiveness in others c) become exhausted d) feel isolated.

Resistance is always Futile as it only Sustains Your Suffering

Whenever anger appears on the horizon of your consciousness, you will notice that you are in a state of resistance, or non-acceptance, towards an event, a set of circumstance or the other person - sometimes all three. Resistance is the seed of all conflict between people and between nations. Resistance sustains the cycle of violence with others and with yourself, and it is driven by the emotions of fear and anger. This is why the first step to resolve all conflict is always acceptance. It is to accept the past is past and nothing can change it. It is to accept that other people's behaviour cannot be controlled, because you cannot control their thoughts and decisions, and you definitely cannot control their beliefs and perceptions. Acceptance ensures that our mind does not become shrouded in red mist. If Rusedski had simply accepted the umpire's decision and moved on, he would not have lost the plot. That does not mean he has no right to challenge the call. Challenge by all means. But anger is not required to challenge something. In fact, if anger is used, then it's ninety nine percent certain that resistance will be the reply. Not to mention the need to heal yet another self-inflicted emotional wound.

Acceptance means that you are able to think calmly, see clearly, create options and make better decisions. Acceptance is the first step out of anger, out of your self-inflicted pain and suffering, and into peace. For decades the IRA and the British Government were in an absolute state of resistance towards each other. Anger killed thousands on both sides. Then came John Major, who basically said, "Let's simply accept that they exist, they have a point of view, we don't agree with it, but let's accept that they have one." This was the first step towards a dialogue, which we came to know as a 'peace process'. Slow as it was, imperfect as it still is, it beats the violence of anger and its explosive expressions hands down. Acceptance does not mean agreement or the condoning of others' behaviour. Implicit in acceptance is the understanding that you cannot control others but you can influence, and the first step of influence in any relationship is acceptance. The second step is to build trust. Anger is simply a sign that you have not yet recognised the wisdom and the way to take those first steps.

While he started out as an angry young man, Gandhi encountered and absorbed great wisdom along the way. Ultimately his way of catalysing change in the world was through non-violence. Which is another way of saying non-anger. His wisdom was encapsulated in his immortal line, "You must be the change you want to see in the world." And as he walked his talk, he accepted the way things were. He had a clear vision of a different way, but he knew he could not force it to happen. He didn't just lie down and let the world walk all over him. He walked in peace, talked in peace, met others in peace, and eventually the wisdom which emerged from his non-violent intellect attracted hundreds of thousands, influenced the hearts and minds of politicians, and shaped the destiny of a nation. One of the primary expressions of that inner peace was his infinite patience. He didn't do war because he didn't do anger. And the world changed big time.

"I was so deeply insulted and hurt by what you said"
No you weren't! You hurt yourself. You insulted yourself. It's not what others say to you that makes you feel what you feel, it's what you do with what others say to you that results in you creating the feeling that you feel! If you call me stupid that's your perception of me but it's not my perception of me. I know I am not stupid. I can only conclude that either you don't know me very well, or you have not yet learned to separate the person from their behaviour, or you yourself are thinking and feeling negative for some reason and you are projecting it onto me. Do you not remember that little playground rhyme 'sticks and stones'? Wake up, smell the coffee... ultimately no one can insult you, and no one 'makes' you feel anything.

The Source of all Suffering

Even when you rationally understand the absolute futility of all forms of anger, you may still say, as many do, there are some situations where it is justified. When someone does something that affects you personally, like kill a loved one, destroy years of work, or even runs a coin down the side of your brand new car, it would seem that your anger is justified. But the principles are the same. You are, in your own mind, trying to control and change what you cannot change – the past, or other people, or events more than three and half feet away from you!

So why do you suffer so much when these things that you have brought so close to you are changed or lost? It is because they are too close. When someone damages your car and you suffer it is because you think you are the car! This is the deepest mistake. It is the deepest cause of the suffering called anger. You are not aware of this of course, but if you were to take a moment and see what you were doing in your own mind, you would see you have brought the image of the car up on the screen of your mind. YOU have then gone into that image of the car in your mind, and you have lost your 'sense of self' in the image of the car. In effect you have become identified with the car. So if the car outside is scratched or damaged in any way, it feels like it is happening to you and, as a result, you become disturbed. The disturbance is called anger. In spiritual terms this would be called attachment. Attachment is a mistake we all make within our consciousness and it creates what is known as ego. From a spiritual point of view, ego is the root of all suffering, and all suffering can be found and felt at an emotional level in the various forms of fear, anger and sadness.

When you see this regularly occurring within your consciousness, you will see exactly where your anger is coming from, and then you can fix it. The solution is simple because the truth is simple. If you don't want to suffer from fear or anger don't get attached to anything or anyone, to any expectation, any item, any particular outcome. Don't lose your sense of self in something you are not. That does not mean you shouldn't have a car and other possessions. It does not mean you can't have people around you that you love. Nor does it mean you don't have expectations, goals, etc. You do. But your relationship with them changes. Detachment means you are no longer dependent on any of them for your peace and happiness. You choose to be peaceful and content anyway. So when cars get scratched and damaged (which is inevitable) and when people leave or die (which is inevitable) or when expectations are not met (which is inevitable), you don't lose the plot. You have realised everything in life comes and goes, everything decays, every dynamic process is unpredictable and uncontrollable, and must end. Stuff happens! You know this is a reality. Every time you get angry it means you are having an argument with this reality. Once again, not exactly a very enlightened way to live.

Early on, during my own spiritual quest, I kept encountering the idea that 'what is, is'. Though it sounded neat, I just could not fathom the meaning or see what some called the 'profound significance' of this simple phrase. Then one day the penny dropped. I realised I had spent ninety nine percent of my life trying to change what can never, ever be changed...what is. What is, is the way things are now ... right now. Not only can you not change the past, but you can do nothing about what is right now, anywhere. When you truly see this your peace and serenity return, and that's what then positively influences what will be. The only problem with this is that I still keep picking up that penny and forgetting what is, is. I still keep falling asleep and raging against what is. Although I do it much less than before, I have come to call it my 'living nightmare' and it is entirely in my head. It is the nightmare we all learn to create for ourselves and then teach our children to do the same. That's why if you ask anyone who walks an authentic spiritual path what is their deepest effort, they will tell you in their own words, that they have to keep re-dropping that penny a hundred times a day! In the world outside you, in the world around you, even in the world within your consciousness right now...what is, simply is. Can you see it? Can you accept it?

National Health Service or Self Wellness System?

While any form of physical pain is unpleasant, the route of suffering is always downward — from spiritual to mental to physical. Many, if not all physical diseases, will have their roots in mental/emotional disease, which always has its source in some form of spiritual malaise. An unhappy soul creates negative thoughts, generating unhealthy emotions, which weaken the body's immune system. So who is the only person who can make YOU well and maintain your well-being?

Why is Everyone Crying?

Even now, you may still want to argue for your anger. Even though you see that it's always self-inflicted. You may look at the world and see so much injustice, so many 'wrongs' happening to other people. You may believe in something called 'righteous anger'. In other words, an anger which is justified by your judgment, an anger that is justified because you are right and punishment should be administered to those who have done wrong. Then we might ask that old but pertinent question, "Did God give you permission to police the universe?" For that is what you are attempting to do when you become righteously angry and angrily righteous towards others. In fact, if you could be self aware in that moment, you might see your misplaced identification is not with objects or things, but with the plight of others. You are making yourself a victim on their behalf, and suffering as a result. This kills your effectiveness, as it sabotages your ability to assist those who are suffering because you are suffering yourself. This is like someone who is drunk trying to help someone else who is drunk. Your emotional disturbance destroys your ability to communicate with and positively influence those around you. But most of all, you are doing what you don't want others to do. When you attack someone for attacking someone you are the attacker. In that moment you are being hypocritical. But your anger won't let you see it.

Your so-called 'righteous anger' also shuts down your capacity to empathise and be compassionate – two of the most powerful expressions of the love that always exists within the depth of your heart. And that is what both parties – victim and victimiser – are in need of, empathy and compass Why? Because it's obvious that both are in serious pain.

It's easy to see, hear and identify with the pain of the victim, but not so easy to hear and see the pain of the victimiser. It is a pain based on ignorance and illusion. It is a pain that usually has its roots in a cultural or family conditioning, where ignorance is unknowingly bred and illusions are handed down from generation to generation. It is the illusion that others have what I deserve or want, or that others are in the way of my happiness. The victimiser's pain is made up of jealousy, fear and an absence of self-respect. They then project that pain onto what they see as 'the victim'. When you understand the pain of the

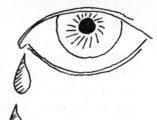

victimiser you find another victim, and yet the very idea of being a victim is in itself another illusion. Ultimately there are no victims, just people to whom life happens. If some great disaster seems to befall you I could say, "Deal with it" or "Get over it" or "Get on with it!". To you, who has learned to see yourself as a victim, it would probably sound cruel and uncaring. Equally if I say, "Aw, poor you", that would sound patronising, plus I'd be empowering your self-created laziness, and affirming your victimhood, neither of which is any help to you. So what else could I say?

Don't we all know that the best thing to say to someone in any form of emotional pain is nothing. Just listening, being present, being available are the best ways to be with someone who is trying to come to terms with their own feelings and emotions. The last thing they need are our emotions, our judgments and our anger on their behalf. Here is an extreme but true story that demonstrates the subtlety of our capacity to serve as helpers and to use the built-in power that we all have to enable others to heal their own pain.

Joe Davis was one of the most violent criminals imprisoned in Canadian jails. Mary Murray was a voluntary worker who ran workshops with prisoners on meditation and positive thinking. Joe never attended the workshops, but the other prisoners would always talk of his constant rage. Mary decided to meet him on his own. He slowly and reluctantly opened up, and for two hours Mary listened to his entire life story. The next time she went into the prison, she heard he had changed, almost transformed and most of the anger seemed to have gone. The other prisoners asked her how she had done it, what she had said exactly. She said she didn't know and that all she had done was just listen. So they asked him what she had done and his reply was simple, " That was the first time in my life that anyone had truly listened to me and heard my story." (names changed)

Your anger at any apparent injustice is a sign of three blind spots. First, you fail to see that your anger is only adding to the sum of negativity. And two negatives don't make a positive. Second, you are doing what you perceive the victimiser is doing – attacking someone. You have made yourself a victim of the situation and now you are retaliating. Third, you have not yet learned to see that the victimiser's negative behaviour, regardless of its impact on others, is itself simply a cry for wisdom and love. Behind the anger they are mentally saying, "This person is denying me happiness and he should be punished for that". It just means they, and you, have not yet realised that no other person is ever responsible for your happiness. You are. Always.

It's just not possible for you to act with wisdom and give love and be in a state of righteous anger at the same time. In fact your anger is your own cry for wisdom and love. But your self-created emotional disturbance clouds your ability to see what you are doing to your own head and heart. While you are in that emotional state, there is no way you can help the head or the heart of another. However, if someone attempts to tell you all this while you are in the middle of your angry fit, you will likely turn up the volume of your rage even more.

Why are you crying whenever you are emotional, regardless of the emotion? Why is your cry specifically for wisdom and love? Deep down, you know inside that you are deluding yourself. You can't see the delusion clearly. So you are calling out for the wisdom to help you see. In many ways you buy books like this one as a response to your own cry for wisdom. It is the wisdom that reminds you that all is never what it appears to be. Wisdom will also remind you that there is probably a history behind the interaction between the victim and victimiser. If you could see and understand that history, it might show you a deeper and truer meaning of the present situation. Wisdom will also remind you that sometimes the roles of victim and victimiser have been reversed in the past. More often than we would like to believe, the victim is subconsciously choosing and inviting victimisation. They have become so identified with being the victim that they feel lost at the idea of being anything other than the victim. But your anger just won't allow you to see behind appearances. In fact your own anger is a message to the world that you are in pain and that you are therefore the victim. Could that be because that is how you have learned to see yourself? As you observe and judge the relationships and interactions of others, are you aware you are subconsciously interpreting them in such a way that you can emerge your victim self-image and play the role which you have been comfortable in for some time? It's as if you look for any excuse to perceive someone else's words and actions as an attempt to abuse you. It's as if you want to be offended! It has become a perverted comfort zone.

Whenever you become angry you are sabotaging your own capacity to understand yourself and others. Then there is the cry for love. Look at it this way, whenever you see any conflict between other people, you are simply seeing the 'absence of love' in relationship. And the absence of love in any relationship is the simplest definition of human stress. In your righteous anger towards others' relationships (victim/victimiser), you have decided to engage with that relationship, either directly (perhaps they are in the same room) or from a distance, mentally (perhaps something on the news). So what are you bringing to the relationship? Is it anger in the form of disapproval, condemnation, criticism, admonition, or is it love in the form of understanding and compassion, in the form of offering assistance to towards resolution and ideas towards solutions? Only the intention of love has the power to transform perception from condemnation into compassion, and then generate the kind of behaviour that may help others to change themselves. What does a leader choose? You are a leader.

It's just not acceptable!

How often do you hear this phrase in response to an individual's or another nation's behaviour? The cry of indignation sounds like, "How dare they... that's not on...it's just not acceptable!" Well that's tough, because there is no choice. You cannot choose to not accept what has already happened. If you try you are once again attempting the impossible. If you don't choose acceptance it will be chosen for you, and if you have to have it chosen for you it will be a painful, tiring and de-moralising (you'll have to drop your attachment to your morals) journey to that point. Acceptance does not mean that you agree or condone. It just means that you recognise what's done is done, you don't lose your calm and you are able to look forwards not backwards, be proactive not reactive and begin to contribute positive ideas not negative recriminations. Not difficult to choose... is it?

Justice has its Own Journey

Are you naturally aware that true justice is... natural? Are you intuitively aware that justice has its own route, its own pace, its own moment of arrival and its own appropriate impact? We all acknowledge that there is a natural justice built into human affairs when we refer to the idea of karma, when we acknowledge that what we sow is what we will reap, when we recognise that for every action there is an equal and opposite reaction, and when we often say, "What goes around comes around." The moment you become angry towards another person's actions you are telling the world that you cannot wait for justice to arrive, and that you have appointed yourself as police, judge, jury and jailer in order to help it along!

Little do you realise that the anger you experience is in itself justice visiting you! You are the one who is suffering in that moment. You are the one who is getting your own back... literally! You are the one crying. What for? For the wisdom to free you from your ignorance and for the love that may wipe away the inner tears of your unhappiness. But you cannot see the true nature of your cry because you cannot see your anger as a form of suffering. The beliefs that you have been taught, that anger is not only OK but good, are still too powerful.

This does not mean that you just sit idly by watching the persecutors and the persecuted fight it out. You always have choices. You can leave your 'armchair anger' behind and go help, go do something, go offer to make a contribution to improving things in the future. The key word here is 'offer'. You only need to be careful that your offering does not turn into forcing, driven by frustration, as you attempt to take the law into your own hands. If you do decide to leave your 'armchair anger' behind and go do something it might be advisable to wear the peaceful face of compassion and not a face screwed up with condemnation and contempt. The first face is that of the 'possibility of positive influence' (nothing is guaranteed) and the second is that of attempted control. One is enlightened and the other is endarkened. Obviously this is not easy to begin with, especially if it's personal.

All this probably flies in the face of your conditioning, where you may have learned that revenge is an acceptable response. The heroic mythology, which is woven through almost all modern movies, soaps and video games, appears to condone and encourage an anger-driven vengeance. So confused are we that we have almost positioned revenge within the range of what we call human rights. Such is the thickness of the fog that now surrounds this dangerous emotion.

For years, Jo Berry was angry. Her father was killed by Patrick McGhee, the IRA bomber, at the Tory Party Conference in Brighton in 1984. She decided that she had to meet him and she described one particular outcome of their meeting, "I felt downhearted for weeks, and scared. I had begun to understand that when you give up blaming you experience a terrible fear that you are betraying others. Yet I was elated". Eventually they jointly set up Building Bridges for Peace and appeared together on television and at public meetings. In working with her father's killer, she reflects, "I don't want to demonise Pat. I want to listen to him. I want to see his humanity. I don't want to forgive him yet, I want to understand him."

The unfairness of it all

It's easy to see the world as a place of 'haves' and 'have nots'. At a personal level, it is the perception from which jealousy can come, i.e. you have what I want, or what I believe I should have. The ensuing resentment eats away at happiness, and all satisfaction in life disappears. Paradoxically, the more you want what others have, the less you are able to receive. The negative energy of envy, that you emanate when you perceive yourself with less and judge yourself as unfairly treated, will ensure that your ability to attract is continuously weakened. For some people, it's not so personal; it's the seeming unfairness of the disproportionate distribution between the 'haves' and 'have nots' around the world that riles them. Certainly every human being needs the basic physical supplies of food and shelter. However, it is interesting to observe radiantly happy children in an Indian village who have almost nothing but a bowl of rice and a couple of chapattis a day, and the miserable, unhappy faces of children in towns and cities in the so called developed and civilised world, who have everything and live in luxury by comparison. Now who really has and who really has not... really?

The Balancing of the Scales

We all know the law of gravity because it keeps us in our seats. But few of us realise the 'law of gravity' is just one of the laws that are intertwined with the 'law of balance' in the physical world. Gravity ensures everything returns to a state of balance. Too much moisture in the atmosphere and down it will come as rain, rebalancing the atmosphere. Too much tilt on the ocean wave and down it will crash on the beach. The laws of balance can also be found at a mental and spiritual level. Too many angry thoughts of vengeance will either emerge as violent behaviour, and thereby attract violent responses, or, if internalised, will eventually emerge as physical disease, as consciousness seeks a way to eliminate the mental poison and restore balance to the mental and physical system.

Expand this insight out onto the world stage, then watch people, organisations and nations exchanging negative energy and you are watching either a) one side upsetting the balance momentarily, or b) balance being restored, as it must, because it's an unbreakable law. This unbreakable law does not need to be administered or enforced by us or even by a higher power. It is a law that is simply built into the system and dynamics of all human affairs. It administers itself. Understanding that this law is in operation at all times teaches us the wisdom of standing back a little and just watching, not jumping to conclusions, not hurting your self with violent thoughts of what you believe is a justified revenge. Knowing that what goes around comes around doesn't stop us laying down laws within society, it doesn't stop us from relieving the gunman of his gun if he is in the same room (though you will need a good strategy!), but it helps us not to take the law into our own hands. You cannot rush justice. You cannot force the rebalancing of energies at any level in the world. If you attempt to do so it is arrogance and you only upset the balance of your own energies as a result. Even to condemn those who would try to take the law into their own hands is to take the law into your hands! The final course in any meal, including the meal we call life itself, is always called 'just desserts'! What would you prefer, ice cream or sour cream?

What rights?

At the sight of human rights abuse we quickly fan the flames of anger. And if it's our own rights that appear to have been denied we are doubly cross. But wait a minute, what gives us the right to have human rights? What are human rights in truth but simply favours granted by the state or institutions? In fact, in absolute terms, we have no automatic rights, but we do have responsibilities. We have a responsibility to respond to life around us in the most positive way we can, as that creates and sustains a positive and harmonious world. "But wait!" you cry, "What about the right to freedom of speech, freedom of movement, freedom of opportunity?" We'll go on, speak, move, create. "But wait!" you may wail. "What if the government or the institutions won't allow it. What if we are persecuted if we try?" Answer, if you respond out of resistance you only create conflict and strengthen the forces against these kinds of freedoms. Which, by the way, is often exactly what they want you to do. But if you accept things as they are, and focus your time and energy creating a better way, you may, by positive, proactive responses (your ability to respond), create a better way for others as a result. Both Gandhi and Mandela were public figures who knew this, and they did this after they realised resistance was a waste of time. They didn't cry 'victim'. They didn't scream and rage for 'my rights'. They took responsibility for their thoughts, words and actions, knowing exactly what power and what impact they would have. Wake up, smell the herbal tea, you have no natural rights, only some privileges awarded by governments and institutions. But you do have responsibilities. One small responsibility in particular is called 'how I live my life'. How are you living? Everyone is watching. Well, almost everyone!

Don't Feed It!

So how can you free yourself from your habitual patterns of anger, whatever form they may take? Recognising this emotional enemy is the first step. That means cultivating a level of self-awareness, where you are gently, but not tensely, observing your thoughts and feelings as they arise. This simply requires practice over time. Taking absolute responsibility for your anger is the second step. Not so easy if you have spent your life believing that others, events and circumstances cause your anger.

Then, when the anger does come, don't engage with it and feed it, but remember you are not your anger, you are not your emotions; separate yourself from them and return to the centre of your consciousness to reconnect with your inner peace and innate wisdom.

At the very heart of your consciousness there is an inner source of peace that is also your power. Just as there is a place of tranquillity in the middle of a hurricane, so there is a place at the heart of your emotional hurricane where you can always find the peace you need to restore calm, and the power you need to refocus your attention. The method to go there has been practised for thousands of years in the East. It's called meditation.

Once there, and inner peace has been restored, you will also begin to see why you created the anger in the first place. At the heart of your peaceful heart there is an ever-present wisdom which knows. Every human being has this inner resource. However, for most of us it has been suppressed or repressed by our social/educational conditioning and the experiences gathered on life's journey. This innate wisdom knows that anger is unhealthy, irrational and based on the illusion that the world should boogie exactly according to your jazz quartet. If you listen to that voice of wisdom long enough you will see the futility of your angry ways and both the habits and the illusions, upon which your anger is based, will atrophy.

In the meantime it is useful, if not essential, to understand how to make peace and how to be at peace, even when those around you in the world would prefer you to join in their angry ways. In Part 2 we will look more deeply into peace and find it is not a passive state, or a wishy washy idea, but the very power of your being, the power and the strength you need to change the habits of anger and frustration, irritation and resentment. In the meantime, take a few moments to explore some of the following strategies under Four Pathways to Freedom from Anger.

Temper Tantrums

Habits go deep. It's been estimated that eighty percent of our lives are lived by habit. That means somewhere in the past you learned to become easily upset. Probably a parental influence, perhaps some friends at school. Just as you may have enjoyed building with your Lego set as a child, or placing the most pieces into your jigsaw, you built a place for a short temper into your temperament. From there it grew into one of your prized habits! If so, now is the time to dismantle, break apart and rebuild your temperament or your personality. It's much easier than you think and does not require specialist help. It requires only your interest, some understanding and the intention to change how you respond to the world around you. Never believe anyone who says, "I can't change... I've always been like this... this is the personality I was born with." You didn't inherit your current personality, you grew it!

Four Pathways to Freedom from Anger

Path 1

Emotional Mastery

Anger is a self-created disturbance of your inner peace! If you drop the mental attempt to control others and situations, and accept people and the world exactly as you find them at every moment, you will never see the red mist of anger again. Would it were that easy (and for some it is)! In the meantime, most of us have learned and cultivated the deep habit of becoming angry, so perhaps it's time to learn how to deal with it when it does come. Here are five steps that, in time, will help you erase the habit and, in the process, increase the light of understanding.

Step One
Awareness

Learn to become more self-aware and you will start to notice the anger at an earlier stage, e.g. irritation is the first sign that there is a disturbance within your consciousness. When you do start to feel the irritation arising, watch the feeling and then....

Step Two
Acknowledge

Remind yourself that you are fully responsible for the creation of your irritation. It is never the other person or the situation. Be careful not to turn the gun on yourself and become irritated at yourself for becoming irritated!

Step Three
Acceptance

Don't struggle with the irritation. Accept its presence. If you resist it, then it only becomes stronger and you will likely suppress it. Talk to it, smile at it, embrace it, "Hello irritation, so you're back again!" But don't feed it.

Step Four
Ascend

In making conversation with your irritation/anger, you are already in step four, which is to detach and just observe the emotion. Remember, you are not your emotions. All emotion dies under observation. You are the creator and it is your creation. The creator is not the creation. Don't identify with the emotion. Detach from it and observe it.

Step Five
Attune

The quietest place in a hurricane is in the eye of the storm. And so it is with the hurricane of emotion. The quietest place is at the centre, which is the heart of your own consciousness. Learn to go there and you will always find your inner peace and your inner power. The method to attune or 'tune in' to the centre of your self is the oldest in the world. It is meditation. Learn to meditate.

This is not so much a technique but a process of expanding awareness. It is unlikely you will be able go through all five steps in real situations in real time to begin with. To develop your awareness of the process practice in retropsect. Take five minutes at the end of the day, and review your day in the light of the five steps. Your self talk may sound like, "Well I could feel my irritation coming when David walked in, so I was aware. I did acknowledge the irritation, I took responsibility for it, and did not project it on to him. But instead of accepting the presence of the irritation I begin to resist it, and thereby supress it. Now I understand why it just got worse. So tomorrow I will work more on step three and Acceptance"

Crisis of Meaning

In a speedy world we also tend to play fast and loose with words. In so doing they easily lose their meaning. One such loss is when passion is mistaken for anger. Many believe that anger is a sign of passion, usually when taking sides against some injustice or fighting for a cause. But it's not passion, it's just anger. Real passion is enthusiasm, and enthusiasm does not drain, it is stable, it is creative and not destructive, and it is never 'against' anything. Don't confuse passion with anger.

Path 2

Changing the Seven Forms of Anger
Don't suppress, repress or express, but learn to transform

People not only become angry for different reasons, but the anger takes different forms depending on the learned beliefs, past experience and immediate perception. While you practise returning to the true, original, anger-free you, old wounds will continue to throw up different forms of anger within your consciousness, and then through your behaviour. Here are some practical inner exercises and methods you can use to either head them off or begin to heal them.

1 Irritation
You create this when things don't happen fast enough, e.g. when your computer just hangs for a moment, the car in front is a bit slow or someone is tapping a finger in a silent room.

Solution: Cultivate patience and a serene acceptance that everything and everyone has their own rhythm, their own pace of living. And if it's tapping fingers that are bothering you, either start tapping yourself or gently request them to stop tapping.

2 Frustration
You create this when things don't go the way you wanted or expected or envisaged.

Solution: Accept the way things went – embrace, work with and learn from what happened. Accept the way things are. Always respond proactively in the Present, not reactively against the Past. Only then will the future begin to turn out closer to what you envisage.

3 Grudge
You create this when you believe you have been wronged by someone in the past.

Solution: Remember, no one hurts you mei t lly or emotionally. You do it to yourself... always.

4 Resentment

You create this towards those that you think have insulted or offended you.

Solution: It's not others words that hurt, it's what you did with those words in your own mind. We all know a person who is thick skinned. Nothing seems to affect them. Develop a thick skin. Learn to hear but not hear. Imaging the person who is hurling the insults is encased in a glass jar and while you see their lips move you cannot hear their words.

You also create resentment when you are jealous of someone.

Solution: Stop comparing and aspiring to be like someone else. Get on with your own life. You cannot be someone else and no one owes you anything.

5 Contempt

You create this following your judgment and deep disapproval of another's actions.

Solution: Separate the person from the action and remember their actions begin with their beliefs. They have likely learned (like you) the wrong beliefs. Remind yourself that you cannot control others – suspend your judgment. Don't approve or disapprove. Just watch. Then imagine the most proactive response. Then do it.

6 Hate

You create this when you decide someone represents evil or extreme nastiness.

Solution: Notice how you are making yourself an emotional slave to the object of your hate, and that means you are not free, and that means you are unhappy. Remember everyone is intrinsically good, they just forgot. See their hate and their actions as a cry for help, a cry for attention, a cry for love.

7 Rage

You create this following the build up of anger normally in response to others' actions which you deem obstructive or invasive, e.g. road rage.

Solution: It's time to get help, attend a course, get a coach, enter therapy, learn meditation.

The Martyr's Tale

We have all met a martyr. Perhaps you have occasionally played the role yourself. Martyrs do lots of sighing, as they tell their tale of 'woe is me' and recall the insufferable suffering that they have had to suffer! If you get too close, you will get sucked into their melancholy story and their victim mindset. You will notice how you actually begin to believe them and perhaps feel the same way. The moment they sense that they have your ear and your sympathy, they will begin to vent the anger that lies behind all martyr mindsets. It's a simple anger. Even a kind of baby anger, based on, "You are not listening to me". So they will try to invoke your sorrow and your pity to get your attention, and once you are hooked they know they have an audience for their resentments and their perceived injustices. Martyrdom is just attention-seeking as the anger is really just a cry for love, a cry for help. It's hard to see that in the modern terrorist, who martyrs himself for what he sees as a 'worthy cause'. But the cause is just a front for their disconnection from their own heart, their own love. They are confused and stuck in their self-perpetuating confusion. Brainwashed into believing their suffering and death can change the world, it would be harder to be more deluded when honour is mistaken for suicide, when murder is perceived as a gateway to paradise and that people will listen to you once you are not able to say anything. Martyrs don't speak from the grave. And if they could all they would likely say is, "I resented... I despised... I hated...I was angry". Which is really just code for I was lost.

Path 3

The Seven SO WHATS!
How to de-anger your favourite irritants

We all have our favourite trigger scenes and situations where we find a reason to become offended or upset. Perhaps one of these is close to your favourite.

1 So your boss gives the promotion to someone else
So what? You should not have taken it in the first place. Do you realise that you took it before you received it... in your mind. Fatal mistake. Then it feels like you lost it, when you didn't even get it. And sadness usually always turns into anger. Never assume. Never take what you haven't yet got. And when you do get it, don't possess it. It's not yours. Nothing is yours.

2 So your boyfriend/girlfriend, husband/wife has just left you
So what? It's their life, their journey, their choice. Suddenly you made your life, your happiness dependent on them. And then you called it love. But it's not love... it's dependency. And love is not dependent. Love celebrates and supports another but perhaps not their life choices (like joining the suicide brigades). When someone leaves, they don't really leave. You can always send them your best wishes every day. That's love. In which case they are always there. Don't get sad, upset and angry when someone breaks out of your comfort zone. Celebrate and do the same yourself. It's simply an opportunity to break out of your own comfort zone.

3 So your teenage son/daughter is always doing what you don't want them to do
So what? Perhaps they're staying out late, wearing lots of silver things in various body parts, bringing home 'interesting' friends. Can you blame them? What would you do (did you do) if you realised that you don't have to follow the dictates of the resident behaviour police, the in-house control patrol, with whom you have been living all your life? If you don't want your children to grow up to be dictators... don't dictate. Guide, advise, counsel, befriend, comfort, empathise... but

try very hard to give up the illusion that you control your children. You never did and you never will. And if you would like to help them to learn how to do something or behave in a certain way, then do it yourself first... with love. And watch what happens. Besides they are not even YOUR children!

4 So your team got beaten again after a dismal performance

So what? How small is your life when your happiness is dependent on the result of a game played by complete strangers hundreds of miles away? Realise your life is much bigger than a weekly result and a league table. Realise you are here to create your life, not have it created by the games other people play. Wake up, smell the mineral water, see the opportunities, the potential, the unlimited, infinite potential of your own life. Believe me, I know this one intimately, and speak from the experience of someone once emotionally enslaved to a sport and a weekly result. Games are good but there is only one real game in town, and you're in it. You are it. Life.

5 So you were walking innocently down the street and you were mugged and robbed

So what? They may have taken your wallet and other properties but they didn't take away your dignity. If you thought it was taken, you are wrong, you gave it away. Property is almost valueless compared to your dignity and self-respect. In fact when confronted by muggers someone with true dignity, true self-respect, will offer their property on first invitation. All property comes and goes and can be replaced. Dignity, once lost, can never be quite the same again, for a while at least. And if you are angered at the news of someone else being mugged and killed then you will spend your life in the agony of continuous anger and those around you will have to tolerate your negativity. They won't stay for long. Not fair? So what. Remember everything always returns to state of balance and harmony. It's the law of our world. Be wise. See how the law is doing its work. Even when you are being mugged!

6 So a colleague at work is either under-performing or being deliberately obstructive

So what? Let go of your expectation that everyone should perform exactly to specification... your specification. If others' behaviour or non-behaviour bothers you and they know it, guess what? You can be almost certain they will continue to behave that way, as they will be under the illusion that they are controlling your emotional state. It all means you have not yet learned the first principles of relationship building. Respect and appreciation are the foundations of workplace relationships, and if you are upset with anyone it means you are disrespecting and resenting them. So what can you expect in return, but the continuation of what you don't want.

7 So politicians lie

So what? Maybe they do, maybe they don't. If they do they are scared. They're hiding something. They are fearful of losing something, usually power. They have not yet realised they cannot hold on to anything. They have not yet realised honesty begets trust. And if they have, they have not yet found the inner power to 'do honesty'. But now you understand they are a little ignorant. So now you have compassion. Can you also see that if you judge and condemn them, you are projecting your own pain onto them? That's a sure fire sign that you are camouflaging your own guilt at being a liar yourself. You are lying to yourself, but you probably won't see this yet. Actually it's you that's hiding something. Can you see it? Relax. Get wise. It is the most common mistake in the world – but it's only a mistake.

Not Clear?

If you have a specific example of a situation or circumstance that is triggering your anger and would like some similar guidance, or you don't quite understand some of the above advice, please send me an email at mike@relax7.com

Path 4

Chilling Tips!

There are many ways you can help yourself be free of self-manufactured moments of anger. Here is a summary of those covered so far:

1 Acceptance is the Way

Learn to accept everything the way it is and everyone the way they are, right now and at every moment. We'll talk more about this later, but it's good to start practising now. However, there's a good chance this idea by itself may seem to trigger some irritation in you, in which case you'll have much work to do. Are you ready to do that work?

2 Future Focus

Drop the past. The past is like a filing cabinet. When you go to the office do you spend the day in the filing cabinet? Begin to notice every time you go into the past. Start by becoming aware of your conversations and how eighty percent of the content is focused on the past. Consciously but gently shift your focus to the future in everything you think and say. But not a future filled with desires, expectations and must haves. Make it a future you simply see as everything going well.

3 Watch and Wait and Read

As you watch the news, trace any conflict situation that you see back to someone's anger. Then see if you can see why they are making themselves angry. Don't judge them and definitely don't condemn anyone for anything. This helps you build understanding of your self and others. It helps you to see the underlying truth of everything within everyone. Don't jump to conclusions. There are no conclusions, just the shifting sands of change. In the sands, there are patterns, always patterns. Learn to read the patterns.

4 Self-Counselling

Stop hurting yourself, for that is what you do when you get upset about anything. Imagine counselling someone who is determined to harm themselves. What would you say? How would you understand them? How would you 'lead' them away from harming themselves?

Now counsel yourself out of the habit of emotional self-harm. What would that conversation sound like? Have a scribble.

5 Withdraw when appropriate – even when you are still there

In the meeting, in the kitchen, in the one-to-one at work, choose to remain peaceful yet aware, detached yet available, disengaged yet proactively involved! This means you are the master of your responses. Learn these three inner skills and they will undoubtedly change your life. Visualise them first. Then do tons of practice.

6 Positive Focus

If anger is a deep habit for you, then consciously find an area of life where you can focus your time and energy in positive ways. This is like taking water away from the plant and the plant will begin to atrophy and die. Do the same for the tree of your many anger, irritation and resentment making habits. What can you possibly focus your energy into, that will deny sustenance to your negative habits?

7 Hunt the Cause

Imagine you are the Sherlock Holmes of all human emotion. Whenever any emotion occurs it is up to you to find the cause, the perpetrator of the emotion. You have been hunting the infamous 'anger dealer' for years and you are close to cornering him... or is it a her? A few more pieces of evidence and your case will be watertight. Send the bloodhounds in to sniff out the cause of your anger.

8 Detox

Stop hanging out with toxic people. We make it easier for ourselves to awaken to the truth about anger, and to change our anger habits, by not spending time with those who are almost constantly moaning, complaining, whinging and whining. Send them your good wishes along with your apologies for your absence. Never say why you'd rather be somewhere else. Slip quietly away and fear not what others think of you. That's their business not yours.

The Wrath of the Gods

Let's finish Part 1 with the deepest reasons why you create anger within your consciousness. Anger towards someone or something is a projection of your own suffering, your inner disharmony. Prior to anger, you have judged and condemned someone or something. Why do you judge and condemn, and then project your emotional state? It is a way of avoiding the truth about your own suppressed and repressed feelings of guilt and shame, and a way of avoiding facing and feeling such feelings.

Anger is both a defence against feeling these feelings and a subconsciously motivated catharsis of the pressure that builds up from those feelings over time. Why do we create feelings of guilt? Various reasons. There are two kinds of guilt. First is the guilt that is learned from outside in. The second form of guilt is the message of our conscience, from inside out. Let's do the learned guilt first.

For many young children, the wrath of the gods in their day-to-day life is parental anger. Do you remember it? It's when many of us learned to fear the anger of others. It all starts when mum and/or dad misuse their anger to invoke guilt in the child. Why? Because most parents were children who learned that when they incurred the wrath of their parents that was the moment they 'should' feel guilty. It is a classic case of 'the sins of the mothers and fathers being visited upon their children'. The message is then compounded by parental pleasure when the child expressed their guilt or shame, in whatever form. The parent silently pats themselves on the back and thinks, "Thank goodness I'm getting through, they are learning the error of their ways. I am such a good teacher after all."

In fact, all that has been learned is how to create guilt and shame, two of the most debilitating emotional states. It's not long before the child begins to identify with these inner states, as they become embedded at the heart of their self-image and self-belief. It's therefore not surprising that a lifelong emotional paralysis can easily set into the personality of the child. Then the pain of that guilt and shame will either be hidden by patterns of suppression or projected outwards as anger towards others, probably in the playground, perhaps as a member of a teenage gang, and eventually as the 'difficult employee' in the workplace. When this early emotional distortion does not express in overt violence, it is likely to be eating away at self-respect and self-esteem, in much the same way that those often fatal, viral infections eat away the internal organs of the body. Over time, it will prove fatal to the ability to manage oneself and relate openly and freely to others. It may also sabotage potential achievement, despite any skills or talents that have been developed.

To use anger to attempt to make another feel guilt is, in itself, one of the most prevalent forms of violence. Parents attempt to manipulate, managers attempt to motivate and religious institutions attempt to control by using anger, totally unaware they are being violent. Your religious conditioning may have convinced you that you will incur the wrath of God because you are a natural born sinner and, just by being present on this earth, you are guilty, and if you have the slightest desirous, lustful or negative thought towards anyone then you should be ashamed of yourself. And if overt anger is not employed to invoke those feelings then milder versions such as visible disapproval, in the form of 'the look', can be enough to trigger the cowering guilt and shame in another, thereby achieving a kind of obedience.

Ultimately, using anger to invoke guilt is a sign of lazy parenting; lazy managing in an organisation; a lazy and therefore unenlightened practice in a religious institution. Using anger as an attempt to make another feel guilty, and therefore feel bad, simply pulls the rug from under the relationship, driving both parties apart. And yet, in some organisations and countries, it appears to be culturally acceptable. Somewhere in the past, guilt and shame have been perceived as healthy emotions. Perhaps it's because there is an unspoken belief that subtle revenge driven by emotional manipulation is acceptable. The creator and user of anger to invoke guilt is deluding themselves when they say, "You made me suffer (upset) and so I am going to make you suffer (guilt)." The only solution, is the spiritual solution which, as we have already seen, is to realise that no one ever 'makes' you upset. Once realised, the games of emotional blackmail can end, and both parties are able to stand in their power and end their self-sabotage. One will usually have to take the lead.

On the other hand, the feeling of guilt that comes from your conscience is what you could call a healthier guilt. It comes to tell you that you have acted against the law. Not the laws of society, but the laws of life. There are invisible laws, at a spiritual level, that govern our lives. One such law is the law of love. When you are living in harmony with the law of love, then you have an awareness of the unity of everything. Why? Because unity is the condition of love. Love unites. When you lose this awareness of unity, it's as if you stop being, intending, thinking and acting in harmony with the law. And your conscience knows it. It's as if you are going against the grain. You know it. You feel it. And the message is a kind of guiltiness that is more subtle, and not as uncomfortable, as the learned guilt.

When you think or say something negative to someone, it's as if you are creating a separation between you and them. You are breaking the natural union/love between two beings. That's why your conscience may 'bite' a little afterwards, as it sends you a message of 'regret' to say that you have just attempted to break the law. If you do this too often, and for too long, i.e. ignore the voice of your conscience, you will lose your bearings in relation to the laws of love and life. You will find it progressively harder to know and do the right thing. Feelings of guilt will then build up within your subconscious from both externally learned guilt, and this internally created guilt, and you will begin to develop your self-image around, "I am a guilty and shameful person." This in itself goes against the truth of who you really are at the deepest level, the spiritual level, and therefore compounds itself. Suddenly the pain and sorrow of guilt and shame is a heavy burden within. For some it becomes a burden that does not bear looking at, never mind acknowledging. You may then find yourself creating ways to avoid it, like identifying with some issue of injustice in the world, becoming obsessed by something or someone, or just working too long, too hard and too late. We can be quite creative when we want to avoid.

Whatever the cause of these now subconscious (outside of your day-to-day awareness) feelings, your anger at what you think you see happening in the external world around you becomes another way of defending yourself against having to face and feel these feelings. But in truth they are all based in illusion. It is the illusion that, "I am a BAD person," the illusion that, "I am GUILTY and that I should be ASHAMED of my SELF." No you are not and no you should not! Once again, if I could invite you to look from the spiritual point of view, I might show you that, despite the beliefs that you have learned about your self, the truth is you are always a being who is a source of love, a source of peace, and a source of light in this world. You just temporarily lost that true vision and awareness of your self. How do I know this? I now know myself. I know my true nature is peaceful and loving. I know that I can connect to, and live from, my true nature at will, regardless of what is happening around me. And I now know how I lose that connection. This allows me to understand how others succumb to the same illusions and fall into the same guilt and shame traps. I know how you lost your awareness of your authentic self, and I can point you back to your authentic self. But only point. It takes time to see and understand this, the deepest reason for your anger, in whatever form it emerges. It takes a gentle, patient, inward curiosity and contemplation to see the 'true cause'. As you can see, it's deep, but not too deep to understand and unravel. And when you do, you can help others to do the same. But first, just you!

In the meantime, take a few moments to review and reflect on what you have 'seen' and realised so far in Part 1, by contemplating and answering the questions on the next page.

Once upon a time...

There was a little man who thought he could change the whole world. He huffed and he puffed, and he hooted and hollered as he tried to get other people, and their people, to do the right thing. He wrote letters, raised petitions, led protest marches and he even became a politician! Then one day he realised the world he wanted to change was not the world he needed to change. He wanted to change the world 'out there' little realising that 'out there' was not really out there but 'in here'. He realised the world was quite fine as it was, but that it was his 'seeing' of the world, his perception of the world, that was causing him so much angst, which he then projected out on to others. So he stopped trying to fix the world 'out there', and he focused on his 'in here' perception of the world out there. And when he changed that perception, his inner world changed, and paradoxically the outer world changed. And yes, you guessed, he lived happily ever after.

Please Push the Pause Button

It may help if you were to stop for a moment and respond to these five questions. Take a few moments to reflect on each one.

1 What are the two most important ideas/insights that you have realised after reading the first part of this book?

2 In what specific real life situations, which you are currently facing ,could you use/apply what you have realised?

3 How do you see yourself acting differently in that situation? (Visualise your behaviour very clearly)

4 What specific questions are raised in your mind by what you read in the first section?

5 If there is one insight that you could share with someone immediately, what would it be and with whom?

Why Peace Always Restores
The Surrender to the Solution

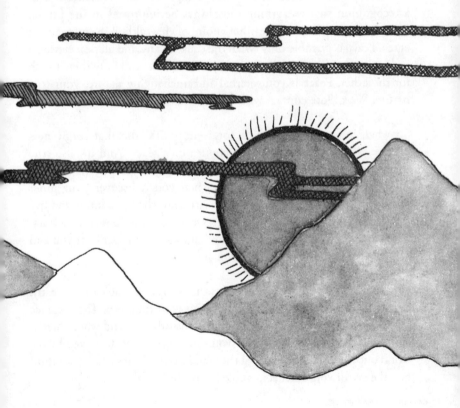

An Eye Opener

Peace is both the heart of your being and the power of your life. If you did not return regularly to your heart, your spiritual heart, to be nourished by your inner peace, you would be permanently exhausted, burnt out, over stimulated, hyperactive, and a real hurry and worry addict. Fortunately you are not yet displaying any of these signs ... are you?

Peace is one of those words that seems to have lost its true meaning, its true significance. Real peace, true peace is not the absence of war or the resolving of conflict between two sides. Authentic peace is a state of being, which shapes a state of mind, which generates positive and focused thinking, which are expressed as proactive attitudes and behaviours.

Peace is an acceptance of the way things are now; balanced with a recognition that everything can always be improved in the future. Peace is an acceptance of the other's point of view, although you may not agree. Peace is possible only when the cause of any and all peacelessness is dissolved within oneself. Peace is personal first, and only then a wish for the other. Peace is your eternal and unchanging nature, your true nature. We all lose contact with our true nature.

So what comes first, peace or forgiveness? It's true that forgiveness of one self and others can bring about inner peace. And it's also true that when you learn to forgive consistently you deepen the quality of your inner peace. It's true that when you rediscover your inner peace, which abides forever in your heart, and when you know and live the truth of that peace, then forgiveness is no longer necessary. Why? Because you will have realised that no one can ever hurt you and therefore disturb the peace that you are.

When you reconnect with your inner peace you are also able to see clearly, not with your two physical eyes, but with your third eye. The presence of peace means the absence of emotional disturbance, and when there is emotional freedom it means that your inner eye is not distracted by the world outside or by memories of the world inside. That's when your third eye, the eye of your intellect, is able to 'see the truth'.

With your mind at peace, and your heart at peace, your eye can then fulfill its true function, which is to discriminate between right and wrong, true and false, and then make high-quality decisions.

Then you are able to discern three things:
1 What is true and false in the world around you – not as a judgment or condemnation – but as insightfulness.
2 What is the right way to be and the right thing to do in day-to-day situations.
3 How to take total responsibility for what you think and feel at all times in all places regardless of the circumstances.

This makes the restoration of inner peace slightly important! So let's do peace first and forgiveness second. Then you can decide which road home you would like to take.

Two Hearts

You have two hearts, one physical and one spiritual. Throughout this book, the heart I mostly refer to is the spiritual heart. Your spiritual heart is really you. It can also be called the soul, which is what you are. As a spiritual being, a soul, you are conscious and aware. You used to be fully conscious and aware of the contents of your heart, which are love and the capacity to be loving at all times, peace and the capacity to be at peace at all times, joy and the capacity to be happy at all times and in all situations. The conscious awareness of your true heart has simply been lost, obscured by an almost total preoccupation and obsession with the external material stuff of life, mostly with your body and other people's bodies. Every single human heart feels as if it is broken and, in many cases, severely wounded. If you go www.relax7.com/articles and read The True Toy Story this will give you a deeper understanding why. In the meantime, a useful practice is to visualise the perfect spiritual heart. What does it feel like, what does it look like and what effect does it have as it touches the world?

Choosing Peace

If anger is the making of war, then peace makes the opposite of war. It is the foundation of personal and collective harmony. It is a clear and simple choice, which lies in the hands of each one us, every moment of every day. Most people would choose a world made of peace but spend most of their time going to war in their own head, and then in their personal relationships. Most people would prefer a life of peace, and many try to build such a life, only to fall under the spell of those old beliefs about how OK it is to be angry, or under the influence of the warmongers around us. Warmongers surround us all, for they are simply those who get angry for the smallest and the largest of reasons. Unaware of the root causes of their anger, they will find a thousand ways to justify it. So deep is their emotional confusion and so powerful is their emotional addiction, they will probably scoff at the idea that anger is a form of powerlessness, while citing peace as a form of weakness.

If you do choose peace in your personal life then you are also choosing freedom from suffering. However, to live that choice and to sustain that choice, it is necessary to rediscover the *location* of your peace, the *true nature* of your peace and *how to use* the power of your peace.

Take a moment to look outwards into the natural world. See the tree, watch the flower, notice the grass. Everything in nature does everything it does naturally and peacefully. Peace is nature's nature. It grows, blooms, decays and dies with peace, in peace. Even the elements are mostly peaceful by nature, until we decide to attempt to control and interfere with their balance and harmony. Now watch the action of human beings. When they do not engage with others, the vast majority, young and old, even in these confused and peaceless times, act peacefully and express their nature, which is peaceful. Their nature finds expression in peaceful thoughts and peaceful actions. People, like nature, are essentially peaceful by nature. Unless of course they have been 'got at' by those perniciously wrong beliefs about anger, which we exposed and explored earlier.

The nature of all things dwells within, and in the case of homo sapiens (that's you and me) that means within your being. The nature of the human being is found within the consciousness of the being. That's you and me again, because we are conscious. To all intents and purposes, the self is consciousness. Most of us have, at some time in our lives (and fortunately it's every day for most of us) experienced, tasted and expressed our peaceful nature. It's so natural, we just don't notice it. What you do notice instantly is when you become unnatural, i.e. stressed, fearful and angry. But these emotional clouds always pass and you eventually return to the seat of your peaceful self. Yes it's true, it does appear that some people are permanently grumpy, uptight and angry at something. Yes some days it does feel as if you are continuously living on the edge and ceaselessly falling into frustration and anger. But even then, away from the spotlights of others' eyes, you will, at some stage, relax into the sanctuary of relief found in your own true nature of peace. At the end of busy days almost everyone goes home, to do what? Sit, relax and be at peace.

In fact, just as you return home at the end of the day, you will keep trying to return to what you intuitively know is true and good, to your own inner peace. It's as if you know that is where you will also find the power of your own life, the power of your own nature. It's as if you intuitively know that your life has no value unless you are at peace within your self. It's as if you know that you can only be powerful when you are first peaceful. It's as if you have always known that inner peace is the absolute foundation for a happy and fulfilled life.

We also know this because most of us have known someone who went about their life peacefully, but not submissively. They lived from their peace, they engaged with others free of fear and anger, and they stayed, by and large, positively peaceful and peacefully positive. We remember that person for much longer than those who always flew off the handle and allowed that red mist to cloud their vision. The peace of another makes a deeper and more lasting impression. All they think and do is naturally positive and good. And when we are in the presence of someone who is genuinely positive and good, we are always inclined to allow them into our lives more and for longer. Which is why they are able to leave wider and deeper footprints in our hearts.

So peace is the essential nature of nature, and the true, underlying, original nature of the human being. But if peace is our true nature, if peace is always ever present at the core of your 'self', why do you not know it, why do you not feel it and why do you not use it a lot more?

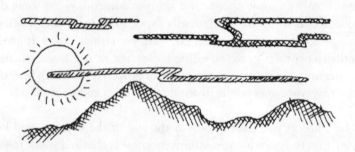

Why We Don't Feel Our Own Peacefulness

Before we polluted the eco and bio systems of the world we allowed certain pollutants to cloud and poison the systems of our consciousness. This had nothing to do with industrial effluents but everything to do with the effluent of multiple identities.

Everything starts new, pure and fresh, and just as nature was once one hundred percent new and perfect, so our consciousness was once pure and perfect. And a pure consciousness knows itself only as it truly is, as its self! The primary trait or the original condition of a pure consciousness, a pure self, is peace. This wholeness or internal oneness of self also meant there was no confusion about anything, most especially about 'who I am'. Somewhere along the line of the past, we began to identify with what we are not, starting with our own physical form, and then with external things like lands, positions, possessions and people. This multiplication of identities sent a series of fault lines through our inner sense of wholeness, triggering the first illusions and generating the first confusions. In those moments, our inner peace was broken, lost in clouds of multidirectional, worried thinking and emotional storms, all shaped by different identities. This is why today so many people suffer from an identity crisis, but are so accustomed to living in this crisis that they are barely aware that it is a crisis. They are unsure what they should be. They are constantly comparing themselves with others. They regularly aspire to be like others. They even imitate the lifestyles of others: all signs that they don't know who or what they are. And if they think they are sure about who they are, the stability it brings does not last for long, as it is almost always based on 'something' external to the 'self', something that must therefore be subject to change. In other words each and every one of us has learned to identify with something we are not.

This loss of true self-identity, at the most profound level, the spiritual level, is what gives rise to fear. And when what we fear might happen actually does happen, we get angry and try to control what we cannot control, so that it doesn't happen again.

The moment the self loses awareness of 'true self', it loses its sense of self in something that it is not. The journey away from self takes us all into a personal identity crisis, which then becomes a collective identity crisis. This is what causes all suffering and all peacelessness, in both our internal and external worlds. It shows up on the surface of life in a multitude of ways, such as addiction, abuse, dependency and neediness, which are ways of attempting to dull the emotional pain caused by our identity crisis.

We just don't know who we are and what we are. It's as if we have all been on a long journey and we have all travelled far into a jungle of confusion. We are perplexed, struggling to find clarity and solutions to our current and now obvious globally peaceless predicament. As a result we have collectively created an extremely fearful, angry and peaceless world. Our inner confusion and our common illusions are simply reflected by the current state of world, and the state of human relationships in the world.

However it's not all bad news. The good news is that the original self, and its pure and peaceful nature, exists within each of us. We all retain our original core, where the inner landscape and the light that illuminates that landscape, is forever peaceful. Reaching that landscape is the only journey of one second and no distance. The method you now know is meditation.

Meditation is not a denial or avoidance of the way the outer world is. Meditation is a healing process for your inner world. It allows you to dissolve the illusions of your many false identities based on external things like position, power and possessions. It is a process whereby you rediscover your true sense of self as the whole and complete being that you always were. Once that inner work is done, the outer world follows as a reflection of that.

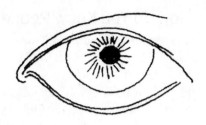

Why Your Identity is Your Destiny

It's surprising how few have fully realised the connection between identity and destiny. It's a simple process to see and understand, even on a daily basis. If you wake up grumpy it means you are seeing yourself as a grumpy being. Perhaps you even think and sometimes say, "I'm grumpy today." It means your self-identity is based on grumpy. So you filter the world through your grumpy filter and the world actually looks like a grumpy place. As a consequence, you think grumpy thoughts, generate a grumpy attitude and give grumpy energy to others. They in turn will likely return grumpy with grumpy and perhaps avoid you altogether. So your destiny of the day becomes .... not so positive! Now translate that same principle and process into life on an almost unlimited scale. Look around outside you now, and you will see a reflection of how you see your self inside. Your circumstances, your relationships and even the events of the day reflect back to you how you see yourself. Are you grumpy?

How do You Know Peace is Already There?

That question should really read, "How do I reconnect with my inner core?" After what can seem like a lifetime of fear, anger and sadness, how do you get to know yourself as an innately peaceful being? How do you know your true nature is peaceful and that your spiritual heart is a source of peace? Only by direct experience, which has been the purpose of meditation for thousands of years. On the meditative journey your attention is consciously withdrawn from all the externals for a period of time, and then focused inwards. As you go into your own consciousness, which really means becoming self-aware, you will encounter some obstacles and distractions which will try to hinder your progress. These include thought patterns that take the form of memories of past experiences, desires for and worries about the future. And then there are the voices of the many beliefs learned from others when you were young. Other subtle inner obstacles include thoughts and feelings shaped by your deeply held habits of identifying your self with things, people and places which you are not. The secret of conquering each of these attempts at halting your return to your heart, to your inner peace, is probably the most important secret in the success of meditation – which is DO NOT ENGAGE with any of them. Meditation is, first and foremost, learning not to engage with your thoughts, but to separate yourself from them, and then just observe them.

Imagine you are walking along a crowded platform in a train station. You know that where you want to go to is the other end of the platform where your train is waiting. You don't stop and talk to anyone on the way. If you did you would be delayed. You would fail to arrive at your train if you engaged with everyone on a platform that is continuously teaming with new people. Meditation is exactly like this. Just as you cannot empty the platform of people just because YOU have a train to catch, you cannot just empty your consciousness of all thoughts just because you want to get to the seat of your inner peace. Not at least until you are a very well practised meditator.

Remind yourself that you are not your thoughts, you are not your feelings, you are not your memories, you are not any of the voices in your head. You are the creator and they your creation, but they are not you. In fact they represent a platform of absolute strangers.

Remind your self that right now you have no regrets or guilt, they are ghosts from the past. And ghosts are not real. Remind yourself that right in this moment now you have absolutely no worries or fears about tomorrow, they are also ghosts inhabiting imagined futures. You are not a ghost, you are very real, and you only inhabit the present moment right now.

As you begin your meditation, be prepared to refuse to engage whenever you are approached by old thoughts and memories. Allow them to pass. As you do you will find yourself becoming calmer and calmer. And it will be as if your inner peace will come to you. It's as if word has spread through the platform of your consciousness that you will not be stopping to talk to anyone on your way. If, with a momentary loss of awareness, you do start engaging and perhaps get lost in a thought, memory or worry, as soon as you become aware of it, disengage and move away. It may even help to say to yourself occasionally, "I am on my way back to the peace that I am." And before you know it, you will realise you have arrived, you are at peace within, and in that moment you will know you are peace. You will be in peace, you will be at peace, you will be peace itself. And it will feel as no other pleasure has felt for a very long time.

Are you there or here or there and there?

Yes it's true, most of us live our life in a state of absence. Most of us go AWOL (absent without leave) hundreds of times a day! Watch your thoughts and you will notice that they either go into the past or into the future. And you allow them to carry you with them. That's why you are seldom truly present, truly here and now, truly in this moment. Most people are totally unaware of this and, as a result, only fully experience a small part of their life. If you learn to meditate, you will learn to be here and now. You will learn to know, feel, see and be at peace, in love, joyful and contented ... now. And in time these feelings will be present for you wherever you are in the world, and during whatever you are doing in the world. Peace, love and contentment are not in the past or the future, they are only and always in the now, only now. If you are not feeling peaceful, loving and contented it just means you are not here and now. It's one of those absolute truths.

Watch Out, Be Aware

When you do arrive and notice yourself being the peaceful being that you are, watch out for the 'ambush', the 'trap' and the common 'mistake' made by all spiritual travellers who meditate their way home.

The Ambush

It will not be long before you are ambushed. Let's say you are the first to discover the luxury compartment on the train. Very quickly, you will be joined by others who have heard of your comfort and want to be with you in the same place. Some may even attempt to unseat you for the long journey ahead. The comfort acts like a magnet. So too will all the old thoughts/memories/worry patterns, feeling somewhat neglected; these thoughts will want to see and feel what you have discovered. Now is the time NOT to ignore them, but to let them come and to look at them in the eyes, and give them your peace. Give each one the gift of your peace. As you do, you will know if your peace is true. If it is, then they will dissolve in the powerful presence of your peacefulness. They will have no power to distract you. If it is not true inner peace they will tempt you and drag you back out onto the platform of your consciouness, which is teaming with hundreds of their companions. Before long you will be lost again in a seething crowd of thoughts. When this happens, don't hit yourself for failing, just turn around and return to your seat; return to your peace.

The Trap

This is the temptation to hold onto the feeling of peace as you try to make the feeling static, fixed and permanent. The moment you do, it will be as if your peace runs away, a little like people do when you try to possess them. Meditation is you, the being of peace, being in peace, feeling your peace, but not trying to hold on to it or indulge in it for its own sake. This is quite subtle, and an art to be mastered as you practice meditation. The moment you try to hold on to anything in life you crush it, you kill it, thereby undoing your inner peacefulness. It is a form of violence. Allow your peaceful feelings to change texture and depth, much like the colours of autumn. Don't expect it, don't judge it and don't attempt to control it. Soon you'll notice your peacefulness lingering longer and becoming deeper. All the while you are fully aware of yourself and the world.

The Mistake

The mistake many make in meditation is one of subtle pride. It's as if we say, "Look at me, I've got the best seat on the train. Look at me I made it to my peace. Didn't I do well?" This of course is one of those old-fashioned self-centred thoughts. As soon as you create it you go against the very grain of your true self, your peace. To go with the grain of truth about peace is to realise your peace is not just for you, it is for the world. It is for giving, for radiating, for transmitting, for sharing. It is a subtle recognition that your peace can only be sustained when you give it to those who are peaceless around you. When you realise this, you will also recognise how the vibration of your peacefulness radiates outwards. When you consciously release your peace to others and to the world, that's when you will feel its power.

Why the peace movement is not really a peace movement

When people get together to create peace, seldom if ever do they succeed. The formation of an organisation or movement is usually stimulated by a common cause against something or someone. It is based on resistance and subtle (and sometimes not so subtle) anger and it therefore only adds to the peacelessness that is already there. There is only one way to bring peace to the world, and it's not by identifying with issues, forming good causes or becoming part of a resistance movement. It's only by being peaceful, thinking peacefully, acting and interacting peacefully. And that means no more resistance, no more protest, no more resentment at all, ever. Oh yes, and total acceptance of the way things are, remember?

Not the way they 'appear' to be, just the way they are! That's easy isn't it?

The 7 Myths About Peace

It's hard for most of us to see that peace is power in a world where power is defined by external position and accumulated property. Inner peace is inner power. To fully understand and experience this, it is useful to first dispel the numerous myths about peace. These myths have emerged to cloud the real meaning of peace and distract us from creating a life based on peaceful living.

Myth ONE

Peace is simply the absence of war

This is obviously not true.
While there may be no wars in the fields or in the air between two countries, there has never been so much conflict across boardroom and breakfast tables worldwide. There has never been so much anger and frustration in human minds. There has never been so much resentment and fear in human hearts. Inner conflict has no borders and boundaries, only states of anxiety, which we become brilliant at expanding, as we feed on the anxieties of others.

Myth TWO

Peace is for wimps!

In fact the opposite is true.
The moment a leader loses their cool, they are no longer an authentic leader. The foundation of effective leadership is the ability to maintain an inner calm, which is then the basis for a positive, open and caring attitude. It is impossible to build relationships with others based on respect and trust if there are not the threads of authentic inner peace holding your personality together. If you are in the habit of losing your cool it's a sign that self-confidence and self-esteem are low. If you feel the need to control and manipulate others to maintain your position, it is a sign that your self-respect and self-worth are low. And if self-esteem and self-respect are low, the ability to give respect to others is almost impossible. You cannot give what you do not have. And if there is no respect and trust for you as a leader, you cannot

lead. Intuitively we know that to lose our peace is to fail, and to fail simply sustains feelings of low self-respect and self-esteem. When William Hague, the former leader of the Conservative Party in the United Kingdom was asked what the most important attribute the new leader of the party would need, he spoke from experience when he said, "The ability to stay calm when all around are panicking."

Myth THREE

Peace is rolling over and allowing others to treat you like a carpet

No it's not. That's submissiveness.
Inner peace is not submissiveness. Once again the opposite is true. Authentic inner peace is the basis of assertiveness. Aggression is the transmission of anger. Submission is the transmission of fear. Anger and fear are the two most common signs of emotional weakness. Peace is strength. Peace is an inner stability in the face of all circumstances, which transmits as acceptance and respect. Fear and anger walk against, whereas peace walks alongside, but is never walked over. Anger sounds like a demand, but peace sounds like a clear and concise request. Fear is easily frightened and looks away, but peace looks straight in the eye, but never stares. Anger is fractious and fear separates; both speak haltingly, seldom listening, but peace makes a connection and communication is always a two-way flow. Fear cannot hear, anger does all the talking, but peace will listen twice as much, as it seeks to understand.

Myth FOUR

Peace means you lost and waved the white flag

Nonsense.
That's for someone who still believes in competition, which is the precursor to conflict and the generator of continuous tension. That's for someone who sustains within themselves the old, small mindset built on the idea that there are winners and losers in life.

This myth is held by someone who has not yet realised that we are all in this game called life together. It is a game where the only enemies are fear and anger themselves. The only thing that is ever lost is our inner peace, our true inner nature, and even then it has not gone anywhere. We only lose our conscious awareness of it as we become too involved, too distracted, too attached and too lost in the world outside our self.

In truth, to be at peace is a victory not a loss. It is a victory over the illusion that we have to struggle, compete and survive our way through our life. Have you had that kind of victory yet? It's personal, it's private and it's one of the most powerful victories of all. It is a victory where no one loses because the moment you regain your inner peace every single person around you, near you and even those who are also very far away from you, are all winners too. They feel your peace and they are nourished by it. You can lose your peace momentarily, but peace never loses you. Some people expand that momentary loss into a lifetime, thinking peace is for losers. At some point, the penny usually drops when they realise that being at peace is the same as standing in your own power. And that is the power which allows you to dispel illusions and change old habits, including all the habits based on the illusion that you have to compete to survive. When you know your self, and you know your peace is your power, survival ceases to be an issue and all competition is seen for what it is – action motivated by fear and greed.

Myth FIVE

You have to isolate yourself from the world to maintain your experience of inner peace

Once again the opposite is true, especially as you begin your journey back to inner peace.
Why? For some time, your lifetime, you have grown accustomed to mental agitation (emotion), distraction and stimulation. Similar to the drug addict who begins a process of detoxification, you will experience an increase in your cravings if you isolate yourself completely from the world that you have used to stimulate yourself (mentally and emotionally). This is also why the new student of meditation often becomes frustrated in their early efforts and even doubts the value of

meditation. In the beginning of their meditation practice, the mental habits of dependency on external stimulation are still strong.

At the start of your journey home to peace, it's best to come and go a little, practise your meditation for a while, then get lost in activity and engagement, go back to meditation for a while, back to action and interaction etc. Just as we learn to drive one hour a day for many days eventually we master the skills of driving. It's harder to master it in 12 consecutive lessons in 12 hours. The concentration and focus of energy required is too intense and after a couple of hours it would become counter-productive. The secret is to do nothing to the extreme. Moderation in all things, even when learning to meditate.

Myth SIX

Real deep inner peace is only possible when you are on your own

This is partially true.
Learning to be at peace within yourself in all situations will require some practice in isolation where you are totally focused on being aware of your 'self'. That's why the occasional retreat is extremely helpful. However, when some hear about this kind of isolation, this self-directed inner focus, they either perceive it as incredibly lonely and therefore fear it, or they see it as a kind of self-obsessed and selfish pursuit. Once again the reality of the experience proves the opposite to be true. When you are truly grounded in your own nature, which is peaceful, you will also 'feel' a tremendously deep and profound connection with others, not just a few family and friends in your own circle, but with the big general 'everyone'. When you rediscover this authentic inner state, not only do you feel the unity of all beings, but you will realise your own energetic relationship with all beings, and therefore your own unique contribution to the peace and harmony of that unity. It is a contribution that is felt to be both a privilege and a responsibility.

Interestingly, if your motive for searching for your inner peace is only so that you personally will feel better in yourself, you will not arrive at this awareness that you are joined at the spiritual hip with all others.

Searching for peace, just so you can feel better, is better than searching for a good night out to raise your mood after a busy crisis-filled day. But the seeking of relief from the pain of your peacelessness, whatever form it takes, will eventually become a barrier in itself. Everything that you currently have in your life, your possessions, your job etc, are not for you, they are for you to use in the service of others. They are gifts that you receive to give to others. It is the same with what you have inside. Your peace is unquestionably yours, it is you, but unless you channel its power and give it away, it will disappear. It is for you to use and, like all things of a spiritual nature, when you use it in the service of others, when you give it away, it increases in depth and therefore quality.

Myth SEVEN

Peace means nothing is happening, it's like a state of inertia

Sorry, but once again it is the opposite.

If you are genuinely residing in your nature, your natural state of inner peace, it means nothing negative is happening within you. It means you are free of all anxiety, desire, fear and worry. You are free of all irritation and anger. It means you are completely open and yet nothing and no one can touch you, harm you or even upset you, regardless of what they say or do. If you are residing in your true inner peace, it means there are no emotional clouds obscuring your inner eye, and you are able to see and understand the depth and significance of all that happens around you. And when you can do all that, then that's when things really do begin to happen. That's when you will know that peace is your power and you will start to use that power in a thousand ways. That's when your life gets started.

Here is one way, perhaps the most important way, to know your peace is your power and how to use that power. It's called creativity.

Imagine you are wandering through the jungle. A tiger jumps out 30 yards ahead. What would you do? What would most people do? Run. Why? Fear. Who creates your fear? The tiger? Or you? In the space of one point five seconds you create an image on the screen of your

mind of your body lying in a pool of blood, and the tiger running off with one of your arms in its mouth. You then use that image to frighten the living daylights out of yourself.

But what else could you do? What might be your options in that moment? You could stand still, you could walk to the side very, very slowly (with a very big clenched teeth grin on your face!), you could climb that tree, you could pick up a stick and get ready to fight, you could roar at the tiger and scare it away.

In every situation in life, there are always four, five or six options as to how you could respond. Why can't you see those options when faced with the tiger, why can't you create the different possibilities? Because you have filled your mind with fear, and thereby lost your peace. You may not have noticed, but it's almost impossible to be creative when you are scared or angry. It is only possible to be positively creative when your consciousness is at peace, when your mind is in a state of peace, when you are in your natural peaceful state.

Not only that, but following the creation of options, sometimes referred to as 'possibility thinking', you will need to assess the quality of each option and make a quick decision, using the eye of your intellect, once again an impossible inner task when fear or anger are present. Your intellect won't work effectively if it's not calm, focused and stable.

So who and what are the tigers in your life? Who simply has to walk in the room and it triggers anxiety, irritation or resentment? Now see your tigers as your teachers. It's as if their presence presses a button in you. They give you an opportunity to realise that you put the button on, not them, and only you can take it off. It's you who kills the peace you need to create and decide. The tigers in your life are an opportunity to practise your peace, to stand in your power and to create a positive, proactive and peaceful response.

Perhaps, like many others, you have not yet noticed the purpose of life is to be creative. The deepest joy in life comes when you are being creative in a purposeful way. You didn't come here to 'get a life' you came to create your life. That means creativity is the one thing you are doing all the time. If you take a moment you will see this is true, simply by virtue of the fact that you think. Everything in your life is a result of your thinking. The quality of your thinking is dependent on one thing, the quality of your consciousness. Thoughts, choices, decisions, and therefore your destiny, all flow from your state of consciousness. If peace is the basis of your state, and you learn to reside in that state at all times, in all circumstances, you will give yourself the best chance to create a positive destiny in the form of a happy and contented life. But if you allow anger or fear to interfere with your life creation on a daily basis, it will shape a destiny that is not what you might consciously choose. Can you see it?

Can you see why inner peace is the basis of everything you create? You haven't forgotten that you create your own life, have you? You haven't fallen back under the old fatal belief that it's 'them' that shapes your life, it's circumstances, it's events, it's my parents, it's the government, it's just fate that does it for me. All those things make up the very real 'context' of your life, but they don't create your destiny. They may shape your destiny, but only to the extent that you let them. Your destiny will be defined by how you respond to life around you, and your response is always completely your responsibility. When you do truly see this, you will be free again. It can look like hard work, especially when you have been conditioned to believe it's 'them', and not you, that creates your life; but this is the ultimate freedom. Make peace with this truth, be a humble student and re-lay your inner foundation of deep, inner peace. Then learn to think and act from that peace. Learn quietly, learn eagerly, learn inwardly to take responsibility for your experience of every moment of every day.

Quick Thinking from a Present Mind

Many years ago a friend of mine was walking home late at night through the streets and alleyways of New York. As he walked down one alley, he was approached by three young men. He could tell from their body language and attitude that he was about to be mugged. As they came close, he put up his hands and said, "Wait, I want to sing and dance for you." With his three would-be muggers somewhat startled and thrown slightly off balance, he started to sing and dance. As he did he gradually moved towards them, and then slowly away from them, and then close to them, and then away from them. In the second 'away' movement he stopped singing and ran down the alley and escaped. Now wasn't that cool! How could he do that in a situation where most of us would be paralysed by fear? He had what some would call presence of mind, or peace in his mind, which allowed him to create and enact an instant strategy that possibly saved him from a lot of physical pain. He had been a daily meditator for over twenty years.

Making Peace

I'd like to make some assumptions. I'm going to assume that you now understand the irrationality, futility and the insanity of anger. I am going to assume that you are now more aware, more open, more accepting of the idea that peace is your nature and that, when you are at peace within yourself, you are potentially at your most powerful, your most creative. How do you find this peace, be in this peace, make this inner peace real in your life?

I am sure I told you nothing new when I said earlier that the oldest and most effective method is meditation. However, if that is true you may say, "Well, if meditation is such an effective way to find peace in life why is it so very few people are actually doing it?" There are a number of answers to this.

1 False Peace

Most people are not peaceless enough to realise they are suffering their way through life and that they can do something about it. As we saw earlier most of us become addicts of some form of external, sense-based stimulation – the stimulation of the media, friends' gossip, another person's personality, a substance or even an achievement. All of these stimulants induce a false sense of peace or contentment, punctuating a stress-filled life like elongated coffee breaks. They are thinking "Why should I meditate to find peace when life's 'coffee breaks' seem to induce it with some regularity? Why sit down and go inside when outside delivers the necessary relief?" Actually that's half the answer, 'relief' is all it is, relief from the pain of peaceless thinking and the rollercoaster of emotions that are inevitable when peace is externally sourced. Eventually the power of stimulated relief wears off and they are left searching for more powerful ways to gain that relief.

Look around you and you will see the compulsive achiever, the obsessive goal setter, the serial gossip peddler, the frantic foodies, the telly-tubbies (the opposite of weight watchers) – all addicted to something that gives them a quick fix of ... phew! The pain of their addiction has not yet reached a level of deep despair which eventually makes them realise their stimulant is not working and is in fact counterproductive, and may eventually kill them. But it will one day. Only then will ideas like meditation, visualisation and self-reflection be allowed through the swing doors of a stress-filled life. It's exactly what happened to me!

2 False Friends

Sometimes people wake up one day and realise they need to go in, not out, to change the quality of their life. So they explore methods of personal development and self-growth that inevitably will bring them to meditation. But as soon as they tell their friends, family or colleagues that they are going to experiment with contemplating life, the universe and everything in a lotus position, it can evoke many strange images and they are scoffed at, possibly ridiculed and may be on the end of a continuous ribbing. They begin to believe what they hear, that what they are doing is just silly, and so they drop it just to restore some normality to their relationships.

Which is why if you undertake any form of personal development or spiritual practice, it's always best to say nothing to anyone. Just quietly get on with it. People are scared you will change. It means their comfort zone, which includes you living and behaving in ways to which they have becomes accustomed, may have to change. Hence the various ways they may attempt to throw a bucket of cold water over your motivation. Good friends will always support and encourage you. They may even join you. But it's best to 'keep mum' until you are well on your way.

3 False Priorities

And then there are those who try a little meditation and come to the conclusion that just sitting there is a form of doing nothing. They have been taught to believe that life is always about 'doing something'. Unless you're up and out there and at'em, then you're not living. So they conclude that focusing on the inner self truly is a low priority waste of time, while focusing on others and talking about how others should change is a high priority effective investment. They are action addicts, the rushaholics, constantly on the run from themselves. Thereby ends their meditation practice, if they ever did get started. It is highly likely however that one day the engine will come off the rails and they will realise 'being' comes before 'doing', that you can't change how you 'do' your life by talking about how others should do their life. Suddenly new priorities will kick in. And perhaps that may include some daily moments of contemplation and the realisation that roses do exist and are available to be smelled!

4 False Evidence

Whenever you start to meditate seriously, you will be making an inner journey into your own consciousness. You will increase your awareness of what is going on inside your mind, intellect and memory, the three faculties of your consciousness. Just as you might open that cupboard in your home that only gets opened once a year, when you do look inside you see a lot of junk, and a) you do not like the look of it, b) you don't want clean it up and c) it's as if you know that if you start to tidy, start to move stuff, then you will discover even more junk underneath. It all seems too messy, too much like hard work, so better shut the door and make another cup of tea!

And so it is when you truly go inwards. The cupboards of your consciousness will rattle with junk and it's not long before another cup of tea looks like a better way to relax. Which is why it's good to have a meditation teacher. Someone who has cleaned out their own cupboards. Someone who can help you recognise your inner junk and to see that what appears as junk, what appears as negative and dark, isn't really dark at all. They can show you the illusions out of which you create your delusions and confusions. And they know how to dissolve such illusions in an instant. In the beginning at least, it is always advisable to have a meditation teacher helping you. Go find a teacher.

5 False Method

When you learn to meditate, it is possible that the method will be accompanied by some understanding of the self, of consciousness, its role and its purpose. You may find yourself stepping onto a spiritual path with other daily practices that are designed to enhance your meditation practice. This could include aspects of diet, sleeping patterns and perhaps a focus on being of service to others. Then it all may 'seem' like some religious package you are being pressed into buying. It's therefore a good idea to clarify the difference between religion and spirituality. Religion has a tendency to offer a package of beliefs that must be believed, or else there will be certain consequences, whereas spirituality will emphasise a process of personal change, where your own personal experience is the main measure of progress, as opposed to how well you remember and recite the beliefs. When you step onto any spiritual path, or study any spiritual wisdom, the fact that there is a daily meditative practice is one of the signs of the authenticity of the teaching. It means there is an understanding that blind belief is not enough, that only the direct personal experience and realisation through meditative practice can validate that what is taught is true. Here are seven of hundreds of other signs of the authenticity of a spiritual path that would include meditative/contemplative practice:

- the emphasis is on the changing process of personal experience, not a package of static beliefs;
- there is a personal practice that results in self-realisation, i.e. the realisation of who and what I am, as opposed to how I have been taught by others to see myself;
- there is a real positive transformation of thought, attitude and action, that is felt by the self, and is consistently visible to others;
- there is a gradual increase in spiritual power over a long period of time;
- illusions about the self and the world are recognised and progressively dissolve to reveal deeper clarity of understanding;
- those who teach 'the practice' walk their talk and the leaders are held as leaders out of respect and not as an assigned position.
- there is an open acceptance of (while not necessarily an agreement with) the beliefs and ways of others.

Perhaps one more sign – what once seemed complex is not only simplified but is genuinely seen and understood in simple terms. If the wisdom that is shared alongside the meditative practice is essenceful, it is likely to be spiritual. If it journeys away, into expansion and detail, it is likely to be just another philosophy. As you practise meditation, you will naturally develop a keener, more discerning eye for the essence, the truth of things.

6 False Expectations

Don't expect too much too fast. Some people expect to see floods of light, feel the presence of their guardian angel or even have an intimate exchange with God. And when they don't, they get bored, downhearted and discouraged. Other meditators practise for years, and see and feel nothing spiritual in particular, except the gradual and steady deepening of mental clarity, a real sense of the depth of their peaceful nature and a growing inner power which allows them not to lose the plot so often or for so long. Expect nothing and enjoy the fruits of practice whatever their inner texture, shape and colour.

7 False Comparisons

In the beginning at least, only share your experiences with your teacher. Never compare yourself and your experiences with others. There are so many varied factors that influence your meditation, that almost all comparison is a distraction and irrelevant. You are unique, so your 'insperiences' are going to be unique to you. Nothing bad ever happens when you meditate. You may occasionally see, feel or realise not such pleasant feelings or insights into your personality, but that is not bad. It is just what it is. And the fact that you can see and feel whatever it is you see and feel internally just means you are ready to see and feel it, you can handle it. Just remember not to identify with what you see and feel, it's not you. It comes from you but it is not you. You do 'feel' but you are not what you feel. Meditation will help you know this is true.

Meditation is the Way Home

If you think that you want to make this inner journey, if you are ready to look, experiment, explore, face and dissolve the illusions which you have gathered along the way, here are the basic seven steps of meditation on the path back to your own true state of inner peace.

Step ONE

Create a Place of Peace

Dedicate a place or space in your home where you will practise your meditation, even if it's just an armchair. Always use this chair, this space, when you can. In this space, place two or three objects which represent peace to you. Then sit and relax your body.

Step TWO

Define the Space

Take a couple of minutes to create and affirm the mental ground rules. for your meditation space – no thoughts of worry, replaying the past, judging or criticising. Imagine the space is surrounded by an invisible bubble. The moment you step into that bubble you automatically stop worrying, replaying the past, judging and criticising. Whenever you notice yourself falling prey to one of these thought habits simply nudge yourself back to an open inner space, free of these mental urges. Never ever beat yourself up when you do get carried away by any of these thinking patterns. In fact, beating yourself up is another habit that has to go. So that's five inner guidelines for your outer meditation space. Actually, we'd better add catastrophising to the list, and doubting too. A little sign somewhere in your space will help remind you to recognise these patterns as inner obstacles to your meditation practice. Here they are again. The seven habits which can sabotage your meditation and delay the restoration of your inner peace and your inner power:

1 worrying
2 replaying the past
3 judging
4 criticising
5 blaming the self
6 catastrophising
7 doubting

Did I hear you think, "Goodness that's so difficult... that's impossible!"? Be patient with yourself. Practice. To help you recognise the thoughts that kill your peace and positivity, take a moment to write two examples for each of the above categories.

Step THREE

Detach and Observe

Now you are going to consciously withdraw your attention and your energy from the world around you on the outside, and then from the world around you on the inside. First the outside world:

- see the whole world as one big stage;
- you are sitting extremely still in the audience and simply watching people come onto the stage, go across the stage, and then leave the stage;
- whatever they say or do is simply a part that they are enacting, it's neither right nor wrong, good nor bad;
- if you learn to simply 'observe' the world, without getting lost in thoughts about the world, you will find you will see it more clearly, understand others faster and more precisely, and not be so affected by events and changing circumstances;
- as you practise this form of 'detached observation', you will also find it easier to be at peace with the world;
- practise this for a few minutes now.

In the beginning, you may find this challenging because you are already addicted to the noise of worry about the world, judging others in the world and criticising what 'they' do in the world. Remind yourself that these are all self-induced forms of peacelessness, and anger, and a complete waste of time and mental energy because they change absolutely nothing.

This externally directed, detached observation is a preparation for the same stance within your consciousness. This is where you become fully aware that YOU inhabit another world made of thoughts, emotions, memories and desires. So now you are going to do the same with your inner world, the world you create within your consciousness, as you did with the outer world, the world you saw with your physical eyes.

- Just watch, witness, notice, but cease engaging with any thought or feeling, any worry or memory.
- The moment you notice yourself getting lost in thought, pull your self out and return to the stance of the watcher.
- You will need to do this frequently as you learn to disengage and disentangle yourself from your thoughts and feelings.
- The effort always pays off.
- Practice this for a few minutes now.

The fruit of this practice is twofold. First, you will find your conscious self becoming naturally more peaceful, and second, you will begin to 'notice' what you didn't notice before, see what you didn't see before, not with your physical eyes but with the eye of your consciousness, your third eye. You will begin to see what's really going on inside your head, well, not so much your head but inside you, because you are not your head. You will begin to see how so much of your conscious thoughts and feelings are simply bubbling up from your subconscious, and you will laugh as you realise how much stuff is buried 'down there' out of your day-to-day conscious sight.

Meditation makes you conscious of the contents of your subconscious and, as it does, it is cleaning and clearing the junk. Sometimes the junk of negative thoughts and feelings will tumble out like an avalanche, and you might be emotionally bowled over for a while. Just sit with it, it will pass. At other times it will trickle through like shy little mice behind the skirting boards. It takes a little time and practice to clean and tidy those old cupboards around the house, and you just don't know what you will find. It's the same with the inner cupboards within your subconscious. Be patient. Be very patient. Remember, none of your inner junk is more powerful than you. As soon as you look at any of it directly with your inner eye, without fear, without resistance, just looking, it dissolves. At this point it's not necessary to ask why it dissolves, it just does. But the moment you stop observing it and start engaging with it, it starts to grow and become powerful again.

Step FOUR
The Tranquillity of Being

After some time, a feeling of tranquillity will emerge within your consciousness. Enjoy this. It means you are at rest within yourself and, in this state, you are also being refreshed. Remember, don't attempt to grasp at this feeling when it comes. Simply be with it for however long it stays. And when it goes, bid it a fond farewell until the next time. Sometimes it will hit you like a wave after your meditation has finished. Sometimes it will call you to sit quietly, while those around you are chitter chattering. Sometimes it will open your mind, like the parting of the seas, and you will see and feel how powerful and deep you are.

Step FIVE
Serenity of Seeing

Unfortunately you cannot dwell in tranquillity as your life awaits your action and interaction, both of which require your presence and your energy. But before you rise from your meditation space, bring the idea and the image of the bustling and busy world in front of your mind's eye. Now look at the world through the peace of your consciousness and see the world with a serene acceptance that everything 'out there' is flowing exactly as it should. Everything is moving and changing exactly as it is meant to. Everything is as it is. Now you are at peace with the world and ready to engage with the world from a place of inner peace. But don't leave your chair just yet. Stay a moment or two longer. There is an even deeper peace you can know and 'insperience'.

Step SIX
The Gift of Silence

If you can now gently drop all the images and thoughts of the world again, just for a few moments more, and be fully aware of yourself, you may notice a deep silence within. This is not a silence that is simply empty of sound, but a silence that is pregnant with the power of your presence. This is almost the deepest form or state of meditation. You are fully aware of yourself, fully aware of the world, but you are fully in your power. Nothing can touch you; nothing can distract you or drain your energy in any way. It is as if you have focused all your conscious energy into the form of a seed, and everything is now concentrated within that seed. A moment longer and the awareness of any singular moment will disappear and you will feel yourself to be in the timeless state of absolute stillness. This is a profound and powerful state of being, and it means you are on the edge of knowing what it means to be eternal. It means your being has returned from whence it came, from eternity.

Step SEVEN
The Stillness of Eternity

This is one of the deepest promises of the patient and sustained practice of meditation. As your practice of meditation matures, you will easily make the subtle transition from an awareness of movement and change, which defines your sense of time passing, to the timeless, unchanging and still state that lies within the heart, within the core, of every human being. Here is where you will find absolute stillness that is completely free of any sense of separation, completely beyond any awareness of boundaries, barriers and borders. There is no sense of limitation, no desire to act, no craving for anything. In this meditative state, there is an overwhelming awareness of the unity of all things and all beings for all time. There is a recognition that all perception of disunity, fragmentation and separation is illusion. Alongside and within this awareness is a sense of 'real' freedom that you recognise as 'true' freedom. This is the ultimate freedom of spirit. In this truly free and changeless state, you may see the world of people and circumstances around you changing, you may see the world of thoughts and emotions inside you changing, but neither can touch you or move you any longer. There is no past and no future, and yet paradoxically both the past and the future are known. There is only one moment and that moment is now. And it seems to last forever.

The peace of this still and concentrated state is so powerful that it magnetically attracts all surrounding energies to itself. When you return your awareness to the world of action and change, the experience of this state brings with it a new perception of the limitations of life, an absolutely clear awareness of the illusions which now permeate all human relationships, and a whole new way of being in the world. Any form of peacelessness feels impossible. All anger is seen as irrational and insane, all fear completely delusional and implausible, and all sadness and depression gradually become laughable! All are seen for what they are, emotions based on illusion, the illusions of our self-limitations, and the illusions of a self that is trying to define and identify itself with something that it is not, with something in the world of form. By now you know yourself as you truly are, a being beyond form, and you have rediscovered and tasted the profound peace of your true heart. It is a peace that surpasses all other pleasures, and becomes the only pleasure that is not craved.

Surprise Surprise!

Now it would not surprise me if, in reading through these seven steps, you possibly had the thought, "What on earth is this guy on about?", especially if the idea of meditation is fairly new to you. Perhaps you were with me up to step four or five, and then it seemed like we went to another planet. That's understandable, as I describe what seems like another world and another wholly different experience. If that is so, then forget steps five, six and seven for now, and just stay focused on the practice of one to four. Master these first four steps and the journey to the 'other planet' will come in its own time and in its own way! Which reminds me to remind you that when you practice meditation, there are a number of best nots, don't and nevers! The first two you already know:

- best not to have expectations;
- never compare your experience with that of another;
- never try to repeat a meditation experience;
- don't rush yourself into meditation, which is obviously impossible because if you are rushing there is no meditation;
- never try to force yourself to 'be at peace';
- best not to talk about what you experience to anyone unless they ask and you recognise they are genuinely interested;
- don't try to analyse the experience, or judge it as good or bad, but do look at it and ask what it said to you, or meant to you, and then move on.

Here is the sequence again in brief. Write it on a card and carry it in your wallet/bag.

1 Create your space (you can do this wherever you are).
2 Remind yourself of your ground rules (but don't beat yourself up if you break them).
3 Imagine that you are watching the world from afar and notice how small everything becomes.
4 Witness and observe your own thoughts and feelings, and let them become small too.
5 Notice how a quietness gently enters your consciousness and experiences .
6 Don't try to grasp it, just be in it for however long it may last.
7 Consciously send the vibration of your peacefulness to someone in particular or to the world in general.

Perseverance

When you decide to do something new you know it takes practice and perseverance. Do you remember the mantra you learned at your mother's knee – 'practice makes perfect'? Practice plus perseverance plus patience makes perfect. It's exactly the same formula for the art and practice of meditation.

The world will help you

Paradoxically, when you do decide to learn to meditate you will receive invisible help. Though you may not yet realise it we are all connected at a subtle, invisible energy level (never mention this kind of thing to scientists, many don't like it because you just cannot get this kind of energy into a test tube). Today, there are thousands upon thousands of people around the planet meditating and gradually increasing the vibrations of this energy. When you sit to meditate, this higher collective vibration helps you, it helps to pull you up and into that state. That's why the best time to meditate is very early in the morning, when the atmosphere is quiet and clear. It is the time when many meditators are sitting in meditation and also the time to take advantage of this subtle assistance.

And finally, for the more 'religiously' inclined

Many people, whose beliefs and faith are based on a religious teaching or philosophy and who regularly attend religious gatherings and ceremonies, are sometimes suspicious of meditation. They see it as a threat to their faith in God, as it tends to focus attention on the self, and not on God, as the object of their faith. However, many meditators willingly admit that the ultimate aim of their meditation practice is a direct and personal link with God. They remind us that because God is not in this imperfect, corporeal world, not in this limited, physical dimension (if he were he could not be perfect and unlimited and therefore not God), that the only way to connect and communicate with Him/Her is by raising our state of conscious awareness. The purpose of their meditation is the same as we have been exploring here, which is to loosen the grip of 'body consciousness', which is identification with form, and into 'soul consciousness', which is the realisation of the self as a spiritual being. Only then is it possible to receive the invisible, spiritual vibrations of love, light and power, which God, the source of love, light and power, is continuously emanating. This perhaps explains why more and more religious people are integrating a meditative practice, and an inner discipline based on meditation, into their religious practices. They have perhaps recognised that prayer, in the traditional sense, doesn't generate self-realisation or bring about self-transformation.

At the same time, some religious believers have realised their faith is a little blind. Blind faith is to believe but not know, whereas an 'enlightened faith' is to know to a level where belief is no longer necessary. They recognise that meditation is a way to go beyond belief in God into a direct experience of the presence of God, and therefore a growing and expanding knowingness of God. Then the relationship with God is direct and personal, and only then can God be known as He or She really is – a source of very real unlimited and infinite peace, love and truth.

However, for others, just bringing God into the picture can be a spoiler. They have no belief, and perhaps even a conscious or subconscious resistance to any spiritual authority. And that's fine too. God is not compulsory, and the ongoing success and benefit of meditation is not dependent on a belief in God's presence. However, meditation is, as we saw earlier, in its most basic form, the way to increase self-awareness. It therefore helps you to become more aware of your own 'resistances'. Resistance to anything means your mind and heart are closed and locked to whatever you are resisting. If a door to a house is closed and locked, it means no one can get in, but also no one can get out. If your heart and mind are closed, it means no one can get in or out... including yourself. You become a refugee and a prisoner at the same time. Which is why it is always good to resist nothing, no one and no idea. Stay open. But stay awake. The purpose of meditation is to open, awaken and stay awake. Believe nothing, including everything you read here. Don't go away from belief, but go beyond belief, and see if what you believe, or what someone else 'seems' to believe, is true for you, in your own experience, in your life. Stay open, keep your door open, and perhaps God may, one day, just walk through your door. But then again, maybe not!

Seven Daily Applications of Inner Peace

In a world where we are almost constantly bombarded by the aggressive images of the media and marketing industries, it can be truly hard to see how peacefulness can be applied to daily life. Here are seven applications of your inner peace. Each one is also a way of testing and validating the power of your peace in everyday situations.

1 Look and Listen Through the Ears and Eyes of Peace

You may not yet be aware, but we all develop a strong tendency to see and hear through the eyes and ears of the past. Everything that comes into your consciousness from the world outside comes through a filter called perception. This filter is made up of your learned beliefs and gathered experiences of the past. This is why no two people ever hear and see exactly the same thing. The memories and impressions of yesterday distort your interpretations of life today. The only way to perceive events, others and the world as they really are, is to be free of all inner distortion and be at peace. Then, like an empty and clean vessel, you can receive the world, you can embrace others, you can touch and feel others with your inner eyes and ears, and perceive them as they truly are. Yes, it takes practice. It requires the effort of vigilance in every scene and every interaction, "How am I interpreting this? How am I perceiving and interpreting this person's point of view?" No need to become obsessive about this. Simply be a curious spectator of your own perceptions and interpretations, and you will come to see how you distort the world and people to fit your own learned beliefs and desires. As you do, you will begin to see how you create the world you see, and you will... laugh.

So try this today. Be open to everyone and everything. Consciously make the effort not to judge, condemn, criticise or compare yourself with anyone. The moment you 'do' any of these things in your mind you will disturb your own peace, create a separation between you and the other, and give birth to stress. Just be still and watch openly, listen openly, without movement. If you need a visual image to help you, then imagine the flower in the garden, totally open, completely still, yet watching and listening to everything around it. Don't worry about losing your critical faculty of discernment. Paradoxically, you will notice that both your awareness and your discernment become sharper and sharper. Let peace reign in your mind and intellect today, just for one day.

2 Peace is the Power to Influence

You now know that you cannot control another human being. You also know that life is relationship, and that relationship means influence. In fact you could say that a major aspect of your success in life is based on your ability to influence. The mark of a great leader is their ability to influence others. Watch these leaders and you will notice they never lose the plot, they never stray from the point of inner stability in the face of changing circumstances and events, no matter how severe or catastrophic the events are. They never move out of their inner peace. And although you only see that peace on the surface of their personality (through their actions and expressions), the power of their influence at that moment is rooted deep within. It is their peace that allows them access to their inner wisdom. It is their peace that gives them the ability to see and hear clearly, and then make the best decision. It is the power of their peace that creates and shapes the power and the conviction of their communication. No peace, and it would be chaos inside, and we can all recognise someone who is in chaos inside, no matter how well they attempt to disguise it. We have all encountered an individual who was ostensibly the leader, but had little influence over those they led. Why? No self-control. Why? No inner stability. Why? No solid platform of inner peace. Result? No power to influence. And you thought inner peace was boring!

So try this today. Faced with the smallest crisis, even if it's only a crisis in the perception of others, imagine you are a ship anchoring itself in a storm. Send down the anchor of your awareness, through the troubled waters of your consciousness within, and see it penetrate deeply into the ocean floor that is the very ground of your being. There it becomes fixed and firm and, one second later, the peace of your heart courses through the chain and up to the surface of your consciousness, to be seen and felt by others through your eyes, your words and your actions. Then watch how people respond to your cool, calm and genuinely caring attitude and behaviour. Just smile at their invitation to get upset or grumpy in order to 'appear' to be one with them in their peacelessness. Don't do this condescendingly, but with genuine compassion, and offer to assist in any way. Stay chilled and watch how this spreads to help others around you to remain calm and cool.

3 Peace as the Power of Protection

Two things in life are vulnerable to attack, our body and our soul. The body is the physical costume you occupy and the soul is what you are. Most of us are under the illusion that we are our body and, as a consequence, spend most of our lives fearing for our form and taking steps to protect it from disease, decay and attack. However, the very fact that fear is present within our consciousness means we are attacking our own body when we think we are protecting it. You know this is true because all you have to do is create thoughts of fear and you will feel your heart pumping faster, and the adrenaline coursing through your body. In fact the presence of any emotion (love is not an emotion) means you are attacking your body and wounding your self. If someone insults you and you react negatively in any way, it means a number of things. First, you have no protection. Second, your reaction is telling the other that they can hurt you, which in truth, they can't. Three, you are in pain and the creator of the pain is you. So what does protection in such a situation mean? What is a field of protection?

Every one of us is a walking radiator. You are constantly radiating energy out into the world through your attitude. If the energy you radiate is in any way fearful, angry or sad, it is weak energy and it will attract attack. When a dog can smell (sense) fear in the postman, it will attack the postman. In the same way, people around you can sense your emotional state. They can see the buttons that can be pressed and know that when they press them you will react emotionally in some way. We all know this is true because we 'smell' it in others. There is an illusion driving this common form of human interaction. If you react aggressively to someone's attack on you, it seems like a show of strength, but it's not, it's a display of weakness. It means you have lost control of your ship and others sense this, even though they may back off slightly, thereby 'seeming' to confirm that your aggressive response worked.

In truth you show your weakness to others AND you suffer internally both mentally and physically at the hands of your own emotional reaction. So what is strength in such a situation? It is an energy that radiates positivity, confidence and stability. These radiations are only possible when they are plugged into the source of your power, to your inner peace. Just as the light bulb is receiving its power from some far away, out of sight, electricity station, so the radiant energy and expression of your energy, when it is strong and stable, is coming from your inner power station, which is the peace that is always present in your heart. If you are not plugged in to this power, you will have no strength to face insult, no strength to parry criticism and no strength to deflect others' attempts to wind you up.

So try this today. At some stage, someone will send you a negative message, a critical comment, a subtle dig. Imagine it comes towards you as a photon torpedo, but one foot away it encounters a protective force field made up of your radiant power. This is the field of protective energy that is being powered by the might of your inner peace. As the invisible but very real torpedo meets the field, it deflects away and fizzles out against the wall. You remain unmoved and untouched. You glance momentarily but directly into the eyes of the other and, with a quiet and peaceful smile, you send them a mini photon torpedo of your own, carrying a very clear and compassionate message which says, "Nice try."

4 The Power of Peace as a Gift

When colleagues become upset, when the family argues, when friends seek a shoulder on which to deposit their tears, you are surrounded by the suffering that all emotion is. While it's easy to sympathise, easy to join in and affirm their pain, easy to cry together, it doesn't help. It doesn't really support for more than a few moments. Yet the world teaches us to suffer with others, to add to another's tears or another's fears, and the illusion is we will both feel better for it. But it never works, it only serves to add practice time to your ability to create suffering for yourself. What else can you do when anothers' pain comes to visit? How can you help? By giving a gift? A cup of tea? Yes – never goes amiss! Your attention, your ear? Yes. But not for too long, otherwise the story becomes a record and the needle goes round and round. An arm around sagging shoulders? Yes. Comfort and support are love's first moves in times of crisis. But your own sadness and tears, anger and fears, criticisms and judgments? No. It only adds fuel to their emotional fire. It only encourages them to sustain their own suffering. It only spreads the illusion of 'victim' amongst two instead of one.

So what is the right gift to give? Yes, you've guessed, the gift of your peace. The radiant, embracing gift of your strength, upon which the other can momentarily draw, until they recover their own. That means not being disturbed by their emotions, not being moved by their dramatic accounts of whatever happened, not being 'sucked in' to their story, not affirming their suffering. Does it sound a bit cold, a bit ruthless, uncaring? In today's world, against a cultural conditioning that says let's cry together, yes it can appear that way. And it is, if the gift of the power of your inner peace is not given with love. For in such situations, love and peace walk hand in hand, like lovers, like brother and sister. One cannot be authentically present without the other. There cannot be peace without love and there cannot be love without peace. This of course is true at all levels of human relationship.

So try this today. Give the gift of your peace to a friend, a colleague a family member, a stranger. Watch for an emerging opportunity wherever you are, wherever you go, when someone loses the plot and raw emotion is on display. Then use that scene to practise your peace in the presence of their peacelessness. It will feel awkward at first, especially if you are accustomed to sharing anothers' pain. But the moment you do this with real love (not with an "aw, there, there" kind of patronising sympathy) you will experience a mini miracle within the situation. The miracle of your true compassion gives the other both the power and the permission to stop hurting themselves. And like a certain prophet of more ancient times you may be the instrument of a miraculous healing.

5 The Power of Peace in Rest

While you may acknowledge that the day will come when you will 'rest in peace', you may not realise that day will be a thousand times easier if you choose to rest in peace every day before! To rest your body, mind and soul, to rest your actions, thoughts and feelings, to drop the baggage and the burdens of your responsibilities for a few moments every day, allows you to 'rest in your peace', recover the strength of your peace, and then emerge with a fresh focus and a new momentum. In such moments of deep inner rest, you will also learn to see the world for what it truly is. Not as a stressful, frenetic, rush to some imaginary finish line, but a creative and playful adventure of continuous discovery that can only be lived in this moment now.

When you GRIP (go rest in peace) every day, you not only interrupt the autopilot of daily life but you give yourself the chance to see the truth – the truth of life itself, where truth is defined as that which never changes. We are all surrounded and impregnated with eternal unchanging truths, but our lost connections with these truths leave us feeling cast adrift, disharmonious and distant from each other. In moments of GRIP, you will see such truths, e.g. openness and honesty create harmony in relationships, co-operation creates unity, respect for others creates acceptance, trust creates loyalty. These are eternal unbreakable truths in the world of human relationships. You only lose sight of them. When you do realise and reconnect with these and hundreds of other truths, when you live them and therefore give them, your life is transformed. To see them and to live them is impossible unless you begin with the first, the deepest and the most profound truth – peace is what you are. No peace equals no ability to see what is true, equals no change, equals disharmony and results in disconnection.

So try this today. Decide to create two spaces during the day (one in the morning and one in the evening) when you will get a GRIP of yourself, so to speak. For three to five minutes somewhere quiet, where you will not be disturbed, just sit and consciously let go of all that is in your head. It's your meditation time. Be at peace and relax everything for these few moments. Then, for one minute, reflect peacefully on the day so far. If something comes to disturb your peace, allow it to pass, as it is already in the past.

6 The Power of Peace and the Creative Process

Every human being is intrinsically creative, by virtue of the fact that every human being thinks and chooses, discerns and selects the thoughts they would like to manifest in the world. However, the quality of your thoughts is another question. If creativity is a function, then the 'quality' of your creation is a line along which whatever you create may be measured. At one end of the line is low quality thinking/creating, i.e. negative, cruel, angry and ugly thoughts. At the other end of the line is high quality thinking/creating, i.e. positive, compassionate, loving and caring thoughts. If that line were now stood on one end, with the low quality at the bottom and the high quality at the top, and if we could imagine it as a thermometer, with peace as the mercury indicating the level of quality, at what level would you find your thinking/creating?

Inner peace is both the foundation and the sustenance of positive thinking and beautiful thinking. Perhaps the occasional inspirational and insightful thought could be triggered by cruelty or anger, but a steady flow of insight and inspiration is guaranteed when the mind is quiet and peaceful.

Ask a writer why they suffer from bouts of writer's block and most will tell you it is because of distracted attention, obsessive thought patterns or simply an agitated mind that is disturbing their inner peace, not allowing them to concentrate and enter the state of mental flow that generates their creativity.

Take a second glance at works of many modern artists. Do you see something of great beauty or an expression of mental darkness, confusion and fragmentation? Be honest.

Listen to modern music. Are you struck by the beauty of the tones, the subtle harmonies within its structures, or are you shocked and shaken by the edgy, often discordant tune, which is also accompanied by words that express the creator's angst, frustrations and solemnity? Be honest. The purpose is not to criticise, simply to review, to sense the presence of 'quality', or its absence.

The message here is simple – lose touch with your inner peace and the quality of your creativity is degraded, the quality of your expression is distorted and the quality of your life will consequently be polluted. This is not to say that life is always a bowl of cherries when you are 'in your peace'. Wordsworth knew loneliness intimately (as we all probably do even in a crowd) but the nature of his peace, and the peace of his nature, allowed him to behold and celebrate the beauty of the daffodil. Other artists and writers down the other end of the quality spectrum have been seen, and can be seen almost on a daily basis, to self-destruct simply because their deep-rooted peacelessness and miserable inner state has infected their heart, possessed their mind and is reflected in their artistic creativity.

So try this today. When you read the newspaper, look at the billboard, listen to the music, see if you can measure the quality of the creator's peacefulness that lies behind their creation. Remember, don't judge, criticise or condemn it. Just see if you can 'see' it. At the end of the day look back and see your day as a painting, and discern what was the quality of your peace behind the creation of your day. What would be the reading on your inner peace thermometer? Set out tomorrow to see only, and create only, the highest quality of thoughts and images. You are, after all, the artist of your own life.

7 The Power of Peace as Non-violence

Sometimes peace appears to break out between countries and between people. Perhaps a long running conflict has ended, a treaty has been signed, an argument resolved and agreement to disagree has been acknowledged. Apparently peace reigns. But is it real? Is it deep? Is it true peace? If there is still resentment in minds and hearts, if there are still thoughts of hate or revenge, if there is still a barrier to open communication, then real peace has not been established. Violence still rages, even though it is not visible on the streets or audible in words.

True peace is actually impossible until all violence at every level of life has dissolved. Real peace is impossible until all intention, motivation and thoughts are free of any form of animosity towards, or rejection of, another. True peace will only show up if there is complete non-violence towards everyone and everything outside your self, and the end of all self-generated violence (self rejection) towards the self.

In a world where violence is the currency of many parts of society, in a world where people actually learn to criticise then reject themselves as human beings, the individual who lives a non-violent life, and therefore knows the deepest peace, is extremely rare. The community, whose way of life is an expression of absolute non-violence at every level, probably does not exist... yet! This is mainly due to no one really being authentically, consistently grounded in peace. No one has yet learned to think and do everything from their inner peace, so they are not yet able to teach others by the presence of their peace. Perhaps there is such a community somewhere in the world, but as yet, it is still out of sight. But don't let this put you off. Don't use that as an excuse not to start. Don't wait till you've won Wimbledon before you start learning to play tennis! Leaders are those who begin NOW. Why? Because they recognise it is the right thing to do. There is only NOW! And you are the leader.

So try this today. Visualisation is the way to rehearse the future without worrying about the future. If you visualise consistently over time then the vision you create must become a reality. That's another one of those eternal truths. See yourself being totally non-violent towards the world, towards others and towards yourself. See others interacting with you in the same way. Grow and empower this picture regularly on the screen that is your mind, and it will eventually become a reality. It must. It's the law.

From Classroom to Workshop from Being to Doing

In truth you won't really 'learn' very much from the pages of this book, any book, in fact. You only really learn when you actually 'do' what you read. Yes there are some very useful insights, ideas and what may be called 'occasional wisdom', but they have little value until they are actually used and translated into action. Then you know you have learned because you will see and feel the internal transformation of your thoughts and feelings, and others will notice your new responses and behaviours. The book, seminar and lecture are always only a classroom, the place of theory. The real workshop in life is life itself. It can be found in numerous places of action and interaction – the kitchen, the office, the car, the stadium, the meeting, etc. Ultimately, every relationship is a workshop – a context filled with the possibilities and potential of personal learning, changing and growing. That's where you rehearse and practice the 'doing' of the insights and ideas of theory. That's where you can experiment with any idea and insight and thereby change how you 'do life'. And when you do, you will have learned. You already know all that you read here. You just haven't remembered it and learned it ... yet. Which means you haven't done it ...yet. Otherwise it is unlikely you would be interested in the content of this book. The most common question both during and after the book and the seminar is often, "Yes, but how do I do it?" The answer lies in the last two words, "...do it"! The secret is not to ask, "But how can I be patient?", but to just 'be patient'. If you were to analyse patience you would find it is a mix of peace, acceptance and freedom from desire. But don't analyse it, don't even think about it, just decide to 'be it'. Then do the same for peace, for compassion, for understanding, for forgiveness. If that is too big a leap of faith into your own being, then take the slightly slower route. Take five minutes out, and use your creative capacity to visualise. Use the canvas of your mind. See yourself being patient. Don't use lots of thoughts to build the picture of a patient you. Invite your heart, the heart of your being, to make a picture of patience for you. If you can quieten your thoughts, you will begin to see patience, feel patient, and know patience. All you need 'to do' then, is let yourself be patient. Be patient!

Please Push the Pause Button Again

It may help if you were to stop once again for a moment or two and respond to these five questions. Take a few moments to reflect on each one.

1 What are the two most important ideas/insights that you have realised after reading Part 2 of this book?

2 In what specific real life situations which you are currently facing could you use/apply what you have realised?

3 How do you see yourself acting differently in that situation? (Visualise your behaviour very clearly)

4 What specific questions are raised in your mind by what you read in Part 2?

5 If there is one insight that you could share with someone immediately, what would it be and with whom?

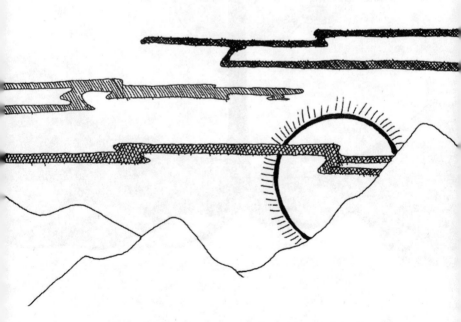

3 Why Forgiveness Always Heals
The Wisdom and the Way

The Way of Wisdom

Authentic forgiveness is an act of pure love based on an absolute truth. The truth that love is what you are. If your heart is not at peace, it means that you are not aware of the absolute truth, so love cannot emerge, and forgiveness is not possible. This is why so many find it so hard to truly, deeply and genuinely forgive. Authentic forgiveness results in forgetting.

The discovery and expression of 'true' love seems to be extremely difficult for most people today. Love is more often confused with desire, attachment and dependency. As a result we misuse the word love and then wonder why we seldom feel the true feeling. To say I love my garden isn't love but the signal of attachment. It's amusing to watch two people say, "I love you", to each other and then, only moments later, see one becoming irritated at some small misdemeanour in the other's behaviour. And then vice versa! Love is never irritated.

True love is only possible when you know the truth about your self. When you know the truth about your self, you know you are spirit not matter, soul not body, and that means you know you are an eternal and imperishable being. It means death is not really death, only a transition. It's not something you hear in school or read in the papers because the opposite is handed down from generation to generation, i.e. physical form is what you are. Only when you know yourself as you are, as spirit or soul, and not form, can you be free of fear (you know you don't die), can you be free of all anger (you know nothing can touch YOU and therefore nothing can hurt you) and can you be free of all sadness and sorrow (you know you cannot lose anything because YOU don't have any 'thing' to lose).

Only when fear, anger and sadness have gone from your heart (from yourself) can the true love that was buried beneath emerge. Let me pause at this point and presume to sense what you are likely to be thinking at this moment. It might sound like this, "Wait a minute, how can that be possible, how can someone reach such an amazing, elevated, enlightened state, where they no longer experience any fear, anger or sadness. Surely that qualifies for a sainthood! There is no way I am becoming a saint!" And you would be right; it is an elevated and enlightened state. While it can be seen as a destination, it is better to describe it as the direction of a journey that you may have sensed as being signposted in the first two parts of this book. The further you travel down this particular road, call it the road of 'increasing awareness and gradual enlightenment', then the less powerful and less frequent becomes your fear, anger and sadness. It is a gradual process. These debilitating emotions are not going to disappear overnight. They won't go until you have learned the lessons they come to show you and teach you. Once again it's the Wimbledon Championships principle. Don't wait to become the world's number one tennis player until you play Wimbledon. How many tennis players have played Wimbledon and become better tennis players for it, got nowhere near winning it and said, "I wouldn't have missed it for the world, and it improved my game immensely"? Thousands. Probably the vast majority. They made the journey anyway.

So what's your journey? What destination are you going to aim for? Will you continue down that road called 'surviving my misery', which is potholed with daily bouts of emotional stress, i.e. a hundred different shades of sadness, anger and fear, shared with your family and friends along the way? Or are you ready to explore a different route, different scenery, different highways and many fascinating byways? I sense you are, otherwise you would not be reading this.

We are each innately loving beings, despite all we may have said or done. We are each a potential source of love in the world at all times and in all places. Most of us are unaware of this truth. We just don't know it because we don't know ourselves. The most obvious sign, that we forget that love is what we are, is when we seek love from others. This comes from the false belief that we need others' love to be happy. Belief is not the truth. Belief replaces truth when truth is lost, and the truth is, love is what you are. However, the moment you desire, expect, complain, criticise or blame, you are not love, you are an embodiment of fear or anger, the opposite of love.

When you are ignorant of the truth that love is what 'I am' and that love is what 'everyone is', you will find it impossible to forgive. When you are ignorant of the fact that love is what you are, you live a needy life, expecting others to supply the love you think you need (which easily turns into "I deserve"), and when you don't get what you believe you deserve (which is really desire in disguise) you become frustrated, angry and hurt. To see, feel and know this truth about your self and others, the first step is to be at peace with yourself and with the world. Which is why peace comes first. In short, peace is, love does, truth guides and forgiveness heals any mistakes on the road called 'increasing awareness and gradual enlightenment'. This is the sequence when you live the right way round, from inside out, not outside in. You cannot forgive unless you are at peace, unless you have realised your highest purpose is to love and the action of your love is guided by truth.

Forgiveness heals all hurt. Authentic forgiveness is only complete when you have left all hurt completely and totally behind – when it truly is forgotten, wiped from the records of your memory. You can keep replaying the past hurts and sustain your pain in the present moment, or you can let go of the past, find peace in the present, know the reality of love, which is truly what you are, and when you do you will have forgiven. To find peace in the present you will need to let go of past pain, which starts with the ending of the repetition of the pain in your own mind.

Three Essential Truths

The power you receive from the realisation of the three following truths is essential help. The *first truth* is that no one else but you created that pain you call hurt. It has always and only ever been you – in truth. Then the *second truth* needs to be applied – it was just a mistake you made – and all human mistakes at a spiritual level can be corrected by the truth, because mistakes are made of illusion, which is a form of ignorance. Then the *third truth* – that it wasn't YOU that was hurt but your ego (the wrong image of yourself) that you created, and your mistake was to remain attached, i.e. identified with that false image of yourself. That's why it felt as if you were affected (hurt) when you perceived something or someone threatening that image. When someone insults your nationality, you feel hurt because you are attached to, and identify with, an image based on your national label. From a spiritual point of view, which means the view of absolute truth, this is insane, because you are not your nationality. The essential and authentic you has no nationality. When you cease to mistake yourself for something you are not, you therefore cease to hurt yourself.

You will find it hard to understand what I just said in the last two paragraphs until you go into your own consciousness and 'see' this process for your self. In truth, the ego is responsible for all human suffering and in truth, the ego is simply human consciousness (the self) identifying with something that it is not. When you watch what is going on inside yourself you will see what you really are and all the things you thought you were and now know you are not. Self-awareness, contemplation and meditation are the keys to seeing this. Not analysis. You don't need to analyse, simply observe. See if you can see within yourself what I have just described. When you do, you will come to know what is true and what is false, what is empowering and what is disempowering. You will then see and know what is the right thing to do. In fact, you already know, it's just that you have forgotten and have not relearned what you know... yet.

So let's do hurt and forgiveness. As we have already established, any form of pain at a physical level, any suffering at a mental/emotional level, will normally be attributed to someone or something else. You might blame another person for not fulfilling what you think are your needs, or the food for not tasting the way you want, or perhaps the team that just beat your team. If you are not feeling hurt then forgiveness is irrelevant. But the truth is that we are all feeling hurt all the time. Even when we think we are not feeling hurt, we are hurting. You may think that is a contradiction or a massively over generalised and judgemental statement! But it's not really when you realise a) everyone – well OK it's likely to be around ninety nine percent of everyone – has forgotten who they are; b) we are all emotionally addicted to some form of fear (the most common form being worry) anger, (the most common form being resentment) and sadness (the most common form being some level of depression). If you are genuinely free of all these emotional forms, every day, then you are well on your way to that sainthood. If you are not, then welcome to emotionholics anonymous!

Even as you watch someone else hurting, you will likely feel the hurt yourself. You probably think that is normal and the right thing to do, the right way to be, in response to the emotional suffering of others. But it's not, it just means you are creating the hurt for yourself, you are mimicking another person's emotional state, feeding your own addiction and then justifying it by saying that it shows that you are understanding and therefore helping the other. It's nonsense. But that's what addicts do, they tell themselves nonsense. Which is why forgiveness is the essential but almost totally missing element of all our lives. Not the forgiveness of others, but forgiveness of yourself, for talking nonsense to yourself!

Flat Lining

Whenever I suggest the possibility of being free of all emotion, a common reaction is often, "Would life not then be boring and colourless with no ups and downs? A kind of flat lining! That sounds like no life to me." Did you have this or a similar thought? The way I am talking about emotions here means love, peace, joy and true happiness are not emotions, they are natural states of being which exist behind, beneath and beyond all emotion. Emotion is an agitation of mind, a disturbance within your consciousness. And when it happens notice you have no control. Love and its many expressions, peace and its many levels, joy and happiness and their many faces are not agitations or disturbances. They are choices, they are states of being which you can choose to create and feel at will, and as you do so your attitude and behaviour will follow accordingly.

The Seven Responses to Hurt

When your pain or suffering seems to have been inflicted by someone or something else, there is a range of seven possible responses to the feelings of hurt that you experience. As we briefly explore the most common to the least common responses, the shallowest to the deepest, see where you lie on that spectrum. Watch also for the deepest meaning of forgiveness. See if you can see how forgiveness is something you don't really have to do, because both your suffering and the apparent cause of your suffering are based on an illusion. See if you can see how the illusions upon which we base our hurt, the feeling of which is very real, are simply aspects of the dream we all live within, the dream we all co-create, the dream we call life on earth.

- **Avenging:** where you want to inflict on the other the pain you have felt yourself, the cause of which you attribute to them.
- **Punishing:** where you wish to take the law into your own hands, even if only at a mental level.
- **Reforming:** where you wish to change another person's personality and behaviour.
- **Forgiving:** where you want to do what you have probably been taught to believe is the right thing to do.
- **Forgetting:** where you want to drop the past at all levels and get on with your life.
- **Karming:** where you recognise and take responsibility for all your hurt because you understand that you always receive the return today of your actions yesterday.
- **Enlightening:** where you realise that YOU were never hurt in the first place.

The FIRST Response to Hurt
Avenging

So you want to get your own back

Heroes have the right to take revenge... justice requires revenge... revenge is the art of administering justice. So says Hollywood. The glorification of the infliction of pain upon others, plus some more, in return for what 'they' seem to have done to us, glamorises anger and revenge. It has made some people very rich in monetary terms, but extremely poor in spiritual terms. Entertainment exploits other people's suffering and uses it to sustain the illusion that other people are responsible for what you feel.

The lesson learned on the streets by each new generation is called 'revenge is best' or don't get mad, get even. Revenge is now perceived by many as the only proper response to others' unkind actions. Everyone's feelings are so easily offended and hurt, not just by the actions of others, but also by their words. In fact, not just words, it's as if many young people learn that if someone looks at them in the wrong way, or for just a moment too long, they have the right to interpret it as an insult and to snarl back and take their revenge. Then it's as if those young, and sometimes not so young people, spend their life looking for reasons to be offended. They look for opportunities to generate anger and give themselves a 'hit' of their emotional drug. Their verbal and non-verbal language embodies the vocabulary of violence and vengeance. Spoiling for a fight they go looking for a reason, an issue, a cause, which they can use to justify striking out. This is a growing trend.

Revenge creates and sustains the cycle of conflict. This is obvious. Whether it's a Punch and Judy show or the numerous interethnic and interreligious conflicts, revenge is perceived as the way to settle the score. But it never does, it only sustains the cycle of violence. This is also obvious. What is not so obvious is that it is driven by an emotional addiction, which is seldom recognised because emotion is so little understood.

Revenge comes in many guises. Often you are not even aware that you are attempting to exact revenge on someone. You may decide to withdraw your co-operation, or perhaps simply ignore someone. These are common forms of revenge in the workplace. You might create some 'negative news' about someone whom you believe has offended you, or you may plot to get your own back by surreptitious means. Whatever you do, it is because, somewhere within your consciousness you are feeling 'miffed' by the actions or words of another, and you cannot see past the idea of 'biffing' back. Miffing and biffing are common currency in modern culture, even amongst those in the highest positions in society, even in the public arena. Even the pages of our daily newspapers are places where the miffed complain and cry victim, and the biffers vent their fury and seek some form of vengeance.

In the cold hard light of day, when all the emotional dust finally settles, almost everyone acknowledges that this is an extremely silly, if not insane, way to live. Even those individuals who tirelessly spoil for a fight get tired and, if pressed in the midst of their tiredness, will admit it's a pretty daft way to interact. But they just don't know any other way, or they are so worried about what others will think and say if they suddenly change their ways. In a hard macho world, it's not easy to dissolve the image of 'tough guy' once it has been created in the minds of others. The habitual response of 'getting your own back' is so deeply ingrained in the culture that it can seem impossible to shift.

The only way to shift this blinding mindset is to awaken to the truth and realise two things. That revenge is another form of self-inflicted pain, it is self abuse. The vengeful only sustain their own suffering. Second, 'they' didn't hurt you in the first place. It was you that hurt you. Not easy to see, even though we covered it earlier, but it will become clearer as we progress through the other six responses. Slowly but surely these truths are seeping back into mainstream areas of life such as education, business and even politics. The only way to speed the 'awakening' process is to live it, and as you live it, you will teach it.

The Look
When you were young did you ever get 'the look'? It was that piercing, withering glance that seemed to enter your heart like a poisoned arrow. Now you know that they did not know they were piercing their own heart. Now you can 'look back' with compassion.

The SECOND Response to Hurt
Punishing

So you think they should be punished

"Let the punishment fit the crime" is the cry of any civilised society. Or so it would appear. But let's face it, is not punishment society's way of dressing up revenge in another guise? Although the justice system is apparently designed to be free of emotional bias, so often it appears that those who seek justice are driven by anger at what's been done and a fear of what might be done. It is a response that says 'they should get what they deserve' and 'out of sight, out of mind'. If ever there was a lazy way to respond to the mistakes of others this is it, the laziest way being the death penalty. And because we all know deep down that it's really revenge disguised as justice, it doesn't work. It seldom changes the kind of character or personality that commits crime and attempts to hurt others. If anything, it encourages and strengthens their resolve to continue straying from what most of us would call a civilised path.

To withdraw from any human being the opportunity to commune with family and friends, to deny someone the opportunity to freely create one's life, to suppress another's freedom to express, is only going to encourage a deeper anger and resentment, even though the committer of the crime knows their incarceration is the result of their unlawful deeds. Unless of course you are as enlightened as Nelson Mandela or Terry Waite. So few are, on both sides of the fence. But let's come back to the role of enlightenment later.

To incarcerate is to say, "You are a criminal, you are rejected and there is no hope for you." This triple condemnation signifies an absence of compassion, and that means a loveless relationship, which means the perfect conditions for the growth of "I couldn't care less....To hell with you....I don't owe you anything...You'll pay for this when I get out" in response to any punishment received.

However, when you understand the emotional addiction of those who would inflict punishment, it's not really surprising to see so many people who still believe that the punishment and isolation of a human being will rectify their behaviour and therefore the beliefs, perceptions and attitudes on which their behaviour is based. It's really just fear disguised as justice.

"Let the punishment fit the crime" is the cry of the righteous. They have not yet realised that there are no crimes. Yes, there are people who have not yet learned to integrate, harmonise, unify, accept others, give love to others. Yes, there are actions based on greed and anger, which come from ignorance. All crime derives from a basic ignorance about how the world works, and how relationships in the world work, which is fundamentally ignorance about 'who I am': it is an ignorance of how the self, the conscious self, works. All crime has its roots in ignorance. Since when was ignorance a crime?

So what is it that is being ignored so that ignorance prevails in the mind of the so-called criminal? Truth is being ignored, but there is no awareness that it's being ignored because so few realise what is true. The criminal mind is being shaped by a set of beliefs that are not the truth, and behaviour emerges from the thoughts based on those beliefs. This is why we all have a criminal mind and we all learn to attempt to break the law, if only at a mental level. On the next page are some of the most common beliefs that can result in criminal thinking and for some, will result in criminal behaviour. Recognise any?

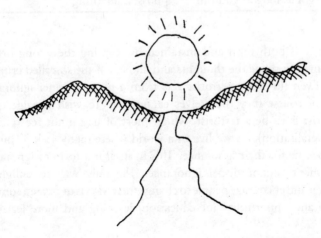

False but Common Societal Beliefs	The Truths
You need what other people have got to make you happy	You can make yourself content wherever you are, whatever you are doing
Other people upset you and other people break your heart	You upset you and your heart feels broken only because what it was attached to was damaged or lost
Success is defined by the acquisition of things and achievement of status	Success is stability of mind and contentment of heart
The more you have, the happier you will be	Real happiness comes from inside out, not outside in
Others should dance to my tune and do what I want them to do	You cannot control any aspect of the consciousness of another human being
You need something 'more' to make your life complete	You are already complete and your life is an opportunity to express it, and as you do express it you will know it
You need to get what you can as fast as you can and keep what you've got as long as you can	What you get is not what you can keep, because in truth you cannot possess anything

Ignorance is both born and sustained by learning the wrong beliefs, which in turn shape the thoughts and choices of the so-called criminal mind. Even the worst terrorist acts from a place of inner ignorance, which of course they themselves cannot see. To wish revenge upon a terrorist is to be a terrorist, which most of us cannot see (pardon my generalisation). So we live in a world where many seek to punish other people for their ignorance. This in itself is a form of ignorance. Punishment cannot dispel ignorance. The only way to enlighten, empower and encourage people to change their ways is to create a context, climate and opportunity for education, learning and more learning.

It's hard for most to see this, never mind accept it. If you cannot see it, let it rest to one side for now.

There are no crimes, just ignorance in action. There are no victims, just those who believe they have been 'wronged'. They too are in a form of ignorance, for they have not yet realised they cannot be wronged by someone else without their permission. But don't tell that to the tabloid writers or those who sustain and are sustained by our 'justice system'.

Please don't...

Please don't read the above as a judgment, it is only a series of reflections. I am still emerging from my own ignorance. I am still learning to understand my self and thereby understand others. I still act out of ignorance. But I am awakening to what is true. I am continually seeing that there is no punishment except the one I inflict on myself when I act from ignorance. If I attempt to inflict revenge and punishment upon others, even if it's just mentally, I generate my own suffering. My own suffering at that moment is simply a message that I am still asleep to the truth.

Please also don't read into the above that I am advocating the dismantling of the justice system. That's not what I am saying. All I seek to do is go behind the surface of things, go beneath the behaviour of some people, go beyond the existing way things appear to be, in order to understand, challenge and find the truth of things. Societies do require laws at this moment in time and space, otherwise anarchy would prevail. It is the steps beyond the enforcement of law that we explore in this the second response to hurt.

The THIRD Response to Hurt

Reforming

So you want to help them to change their ways

When someone does something against the laws of society, or against the laws of harmony in human relationship, it is obviously better and wiser to help that person reform rather than punish them. Most agree that a reformed character is better than the unreformed character who is likely to return to their law breaking and violent ways. The reforming of one's own character traits can be one of the most challenging tasks in the world. It is the underlying purpose of most self-help books. There are many examples of the angry murderer and the violent rapist who genuinely repent and transform their attitudes and behaviour. From a societal and institutional point of view the process needs time, therefore patience, it needs a willingness from both parties, therefore sustained motivation, and it needs the guidance of knowledge and wisdom, therefore an experienced teacher. Time, motivation and good teachers are both expensive and in short supply, which may explain why helping the criminal and the violent to reform is seldom the chosen option in most societies.

However those who would wish to reform others need to be a little careful. If they still believe the 'other' (the criminal) is the cause of their discomfort, then the motive to help the other to reform can be just another form of punishment in disguise. If reforming is an attempt to control another's behaviour, it can be an even more subtle form of revenge.

Perhaps this is why many of those who would like to reform others can become a wee bit too righteous. They develop their own character traits, which lean towards the judgment and criticism of others. Their vision is often looking for someone who needs 'character treatment'. That's why they easily create the habit in themselves of finding fault in others. Like the professional photographer sees and frames their world as a series of possible pictures, the reformer can potentially fall into the trap of seeing others as potential reformees. They look first for what might be the weaknesses and negative traits in the other's character.

Perhaps, after some time the penny drops in the reformer's mind as they realise that it's not the other person who needs to change, it's 'me' who needs to change. It is a truly transformational moment when the reformer wakes up one day and realises, "It's me that's making me offended, insulted, helpless, hopeless, victimised and hurt".

As you watch others in conflict, throwing their emotional pain at each other, even when you watch the criminal rail against society, if you are offended then be aware it's you that's making you offended by their behaviour. The other person is simply saying and doing what they are saying and doing, but it's you that is taking offence, it's you who is creating the feeling of being offended. You are the offender ... of yourself".

In this cloud clearing moment the reformer's attitude and approach can transform. Judgment and condemnation, which may have been disguised as human concern for the well-being of others (which was really a disguise for the desire to 'fix them'), all dissolve. The intention to understand the other suddenly comes from a place of genuine compassion. Like a rose in a garden of weeds, empathy begins to struggle through and find its place in the reformer's repertoire. Then there's another AHA moment as the reformer realises they have just reformed themselves.

Only then can the reformer, who now sees his or her self as less of a reformer and more of an empowerer, be of value to those whose character has simply been shaped by negative influences of the past. They make their new-found wisdom available to those who are still asleep, those still under the spell of the belief that 'crime pays', those still under the illusion that the law of the jungle is the only law, those still ignorant of the fact that they feel the way they feel because of what they have learned. The role of the reformer is then to help those who are asleep to awaken, and unlearn the beliefs which have kept them paralysed in their self-sustaining nightmare of negative thoughts and habitual patterns of violent behaviours.

A few more insights and the reformer may realise that there are no bad people, there are no criminals, only people who believe in their own badness, only people who have lost an inner connection with their innate goodness, only people suffering and acting from their own ignorance of what is true. The reformer may even eventually realise that nothing bad ever happens. There are events, there are actions, there are circumstances, but none of them are bad unless you make it so. And where do we all make it so? In our own mind, by our own judgment. Do you recognise this? Can you see that while the world is 'out there', the world you are responding to is the one you create 'in here'? It's all happening in your own consciousness, in YOU. The world is exactly how you see it. And how you see it is how you create it. How you 'see' the other, is how you create the other. Which is often a million miles from what they actually are.

Yes, there is right and wrong. There is a right way to think and live, which creates and sustains harmony in society, and there are wrong ways to think and live, which temporarily breaks that harmony. Right and wrong are not the same as good and bad. There is no 'bad', if you so decide. There is only our old friend ignorance or... enlightenment. Can you see it?

What you see is what you get!

I will never forget a story I heard at a retreat for prison governors in Oxford many years ago. One governor explained the transformation of a penitentiary in Dade County, Miami. This particular institution had the highest levels of conflict, drug abuse and break-out rates amongst all penitentiaries in the US. In came a new governor, who sent all the managers and staff on a three-day, customer service training course. When they returned he told them, "Now go back in there and treat the prisoners as if they were your customers." To cut a long story very short, two years later the prison had the lowest levels of conflict, drug abuse and break-out rates in the US. Reason? One word. Respect. Instead of seeing the prisoners as low life scum, they saw them as human beings with their own innate but suppressed dignity and worth, and therefore worthy of their respect. It transformed the culture of the institution.

The FOURTH Response to Hurt
Forgiving

So you want to bestow forgiveness and let bygones be bygones

Forgiveness is mostly seen as good in principle but hard to do in practice. It is always easier to forgive your friends when they transgress than it is to forgive someone you don't know. This is sometimes because we are in some way dependent on our friends for approval. If we condemn them, we may lose that approval. In other instances, it's as if friends have earned the right to transgress occasionally... a little! Strangers however, are much easier to judge, condemn and criticise. Have you noticed yet that when you do condemn or criticise you are really projecting your own self-created negative feelings on to them? And like some dogs bark and growl at you only when they are behind their own garden fence, some people feel the distance of unfamiliarity means it's safe to 'have a go'.

To say "I forgive them for the disappointment, sadness and pain they have caused me" is, as we have seen, an unnecessary action based on the illusion that they are the cause of your hurt. Although this is easy to see in theory (for some), it's not so easy to do in practice. For others this approach just doesn't work at all. In fact it sounds like cloud-cuckoo land, especially when something extreme happens. When someone blows up your train on the way to work and you lose an arm, and by the time you get back to work you've lost your job to someone else, and you have to go onto disability benefit, and then you have to sell your house and move your family to another area, to then say "I forgive" to the bomber and your boss will not be easy. It will be even harder for your heart to mean it.

And yet some are able to do this. They do say such words and feel such forgiveness in such extreme cases. They have come to recognise a number of absolute truths about life and human relationships. Here are a few that may be useful.

1 Don't choose victim

Yes, your mental and emotional pain is your response to events, it's your creation. It is a personal choice though you may not see the choice because of the suffering you create within yourself. Chris Moon is a wonderful example of how not to paralyse yourself with victimhood. He lost an arm and a leg during landmine clearing. But he did not stop and think, "I blame the mine ... I blame the people who laid the mine... I blame the manufacturer of the mine... I blame me for not being more careful ...I am a victim." He had a false arm and leg fitted and went on to run four marathons a year including the Sahara.

2 You are not your body

Probably the deepest truth, and therefore the most challenging to work with, is the fact that your physical pain does not belong to you. It belongs to your body and you are not your body. It's your body that communicates with you, and you with it, but YOU are not in pain, your body is. This is why some people's mood, attitude and personality don't change, even when they are physically injured. It's as if they know and act from a deeper place, a truer place, within their authentic self. It's as if they are naturally able to detach themselves from their physical form, while still being in their physical form. For most of us this requires constant practice because we are now so identified with our form we actually believe and think we are our body. Who says, "My body"? You do. So there is you, and then there is your body.

3 Stuff happens!

Stuff happens and sometimes you just might be in the way of stuff happening. That's life. Get over it and move on. If you don't, then you get stuck. The needle of your life gets stuck just like it sometimes did on those old vinyl records we used to play. Then we annoy others as we go around playing our record... "Do you know what happened to me... it was so terrible... so bad, sooo baaaad." As we do, we are quietly sustaining our neediness for the sympathetic attention of others and our addiction to feeling sooo baaaad!

4 Benefit in everything

Some people realise what eventually becomes obvious, which means there is a reason for everything, a lesson in everything and there is some benefit hidden within every event. So they say, "This didn't happen *to* me. It happened *for* me. What's the significance of this event, what is the lesson I can learn?" They take a moment to reflect, look, see, realise, learn, change and move on.

5 Release, let go and be free

If you don't let go of the scene, the event, the sounds and the images of the other person, whom you mistakenly believe 'did you wrong'. If you keep replaying the scene and recreating your negative feelings, it means you are holding on to it all. You are using it to satisfy your emotional addiction. Holding on also means you are carrying one huge inner burden. Burdens make life heavy. Holding on means you are just stuck in an inner 'action replay' mode, and that only deepens your suffering, driving it deeper into the heart of your heart. Isn't that daft. Can you give it up and get on with your life?

6 Forgiveness is personal

Some people find it impossible to dig deep enough into their heart to find forgiveness. Others deem forgiveness as necessary in order to let go and move on. Recently a vicar resigned her post because she could not forgive her daughter's killers in the London Underground bombings. Gee Walker, on the other hand, intellectually walked in the opposite direction when her son Anthony was murdered in a knife attack. She seemed to take the nation's breath away when she forgave the two killers. "I cannot hate. I have to forgive them. Hate is what killed Anthony," she said as both men were given long prison sentences. "Their minds must be very tortured." Amazed by the public reaction to her gesture she explained, "It's obvious that if I did not forgive, and did not answer racism and hate with tolerance and love, it would be an insult to my son's memory." She was honest and clear about her intention to forgive, "In a way I am not doing it for them. I am doing it for me. Unforgiveness is a heavy weight and a load to carry. I've seen what it does to people. They become bitter and angry. I don't want to be a victim twice over."

7 An absolute spiritual truth

From a spiritual point of view (see page 11) there is no need to forgive someone for the loss of a loved one, because you didn't lose them, because they were never yours to lose in the first place. What actually happened was that the moment of their passing on, regardless of the circumstances, was simply the moment they were meant to pass on. You need the spiritual point of view here, because it reminds you that the spirit or soul was simply meant to leave the body in that way at that time and move to the next phase of its own unique and individual journey. Yes, there were reasons why it was that moment and in that way, but we don't need to know those reasons. All we need to do is not identify with their suffering, give them the most positive, loving and supporting energy that we can, and let go. Which means, let them go, when they go. In truth, they have not actually died, only moved on. Does it sound cold and heartless? Actually the opposite is what happens when you live this truth. Instead of being self-consumed by grief your heart is open and free, loving and compassionate. If their departure is not sudden, you can be fully present for them and help them tie a ribbon around their life. If their departure is violent, you can help them not carry thoughts of resentment and vengeance in their heart. And if others are suffering around them, you will be available and able to comfort their heart. There are no accidents or random events in life. And when you do feel sorrow at someone's departure, be honest, who are you really feeling sorry for?

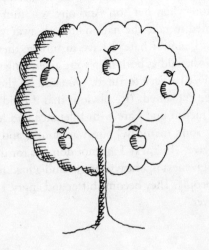

The starving and the homeless

Yes, I thought I heard you asking about the millions of starving and homeless across the world. Are they responsible for their suffering? Should they just sit up and say, "Oh well, stuff happens, let's move on." Their situation is mostly physical. Their situation, which includes some of the people around them who have arrived to help them, conditions them to see themselves as almost entirely helpless victims. The moment they are born, many of them learn both helplessness and hopelessness. And then they become dependent on those charitable people and organisations who attempt to relieve their suffering. It can sound cold and callous to say the same principle applies. Each is still responsible for what they are feeling but they have no idea that they are. They are a million miles from understanding such ideas, such truths. They are simply in need of food and shelter. And most get it. But their real need is seldom met, and that is for knowledge and understanding. It's the old man and fish principle. What's best, to feed the starving man a fish, or teach him how to fish? Millions of moneys and thousands of tons of food went into Ethiopia in 1986, but in the long run it didn't make any difference. That's not bad, it's not good, it's just a fact. Why? Because it only treated the symptoms, not the cause. The cause is always ignorance, even in those with so-called 'power'. The brokers of power, the politicians and tribal leaders, were the real cause of the lack of food and shelter. They too are ignorant of the truth. They too are suffering. While they may have more fish and comfortable shelters, they live a troubled inner life, while many of those who have no fish and no roof, live a more contented and fulfilled life. This is not to say starvation and homelessness is good. Only to say that all is not what is seems and the best remedies are often not so obvious and need to be delivered at deeper and less visible levels.

The FIFTH Response to Hurt
Forgetting

So you want to forget it ever happened

Nice idea, but once again not so easy. Some people seem to be able to do it more easily than others. But 'seem' is the key word' here, as they realise, perhaps years later, that they just stored all the resentment and rage in their subconscious, and then one day out it all comes in a king size rant, or perhaps in the form of something even more pointed!

Animals are extremely good at forgetting, pets especially. Perhaps that's because they have such a deep attachment and dependency on their owner, they kind of know that they cannot afford to remember a trespass. But then some dogs and cats are very good at remembering and attributing their previous pain to their present keeper.

Some say the ultimate forgiveness is to forget. Some hurts seem easy to forget, like someone letting you down, or someone aiming one sarcastic comment too many at your heart. Some hurts seem just too big to forget, like people who appeared to cheat you out of a job, or the killing of a loved one. And then there are societal hurts like war, which appear impossible to forget. Yet it can be a huge breakthrough when you realise that when you don't forget, you repeat! Let's say you do hold on to the illusion that the other person offended you, and thereby caused your negative feelings, can you see that it only happened once, but you have 'action replayed' it on the screen of your mind a hundred, and maybe thousands of times?

Here's the truth of hurt. Well, almost the truth! Every time you think about something hurtful, perhaps something that others said or did, you are only a repeating the moment it happened in your own mind. Let's say you think about it 99 times. The other person only said or did what they did once. But you have done it over and over again in your head 99 times, so who is hurting whom here? You are hurting you.

This is crazy when you see it. This is why you could look out across the world and conclude almost everyone has gone crazy, as you realise that people who are feeling hurt are simply hurting themselves, all the time. This truly is self-harm on a global scale.

So don't harm yourself any more. Drop your pain, drop what you mistakenly believe was the cause of your pain, i.e. the other person's words or actions yesterday. Forgive yourself for holding on to it and hurting yourself, and get on with your life. Let go of all your grievances, large and small. Otherwise you will simply kill yourself from inside out.

During his long meditation under his Bodhi tree, the Buddha realised that the root cause of all suffering was attachment. All human suffering has its origins in attachment. Not external but internal attachment. When people say it's all in the mind, it's true. You become attached to images on the screen of your mind, and when someone touches the externalised form of the image that's on your mind, you become disturbed and you feel that disturbance and you call it pain or suffering. Let's take your child as an example. You are very attached to your child. You have not yet realised that love is not attachment. And when something happens to your child and your child expresses pain, you see it as bad, so you feel bad and then it feels like it's happening to you. But of course it's not.

I'm deliberately using an extreme example here, because it's not easy to just accept and get on with your life if your child appears to be hurt by someone else. But you can if you want to. In fact, you will have to anyway, eventually. It's even likely your child will probably get on with their life before you do! Being detached doesn't mean you don't care. It doesn't mean you just stand by and watch. It just means you don't lose your sense of self in an image of someone else or something else, on the screen of your mind. Then you won't become emotionally disturbed, you won't react negatively when something happens to them. You will then be able to stay calm and be fully available to help them get through their experience. It's impossible to get angry or upset, fearful or sad, when you are detached. But if you have become addicted to any of those emotions, you will resist the idea of detachment because you will see it as a threat to your drugs. Yes, it is human nature to be detached, although many would argue the opposite, that it's human nature to be attached. It's natural to be detached, because you cannot be a source of love for others if you are attached. And love is not only your true nature, it's what you are. All attachment blocks your heart and therefore obstructs the flow of your love into the world. If you meditate on this, contemplate on this, you will eventually see it is true. The Buddha was just one of the first few to realise it, and one of even fewer to live it. PS – practicing detachment doesn't suddenly make you a Buddhist. There is no such thing as Buddhist, just a being who is detached, and live according to the Buddhas ideals.

To make matters worse, like many people, not only do you become attached and addicted to the suffering itself, you even begin to identify with and define yourself as a sufferer, as a victim of your self-created pain. Hence the number of people in the world today who call themselves victims, and those who don't say it are probably thinking it. There are no victims, only people who are attached to, and wrongly identifying with, an image that is always self-created in their own mind. This is where ego is born. Ego is the enemy, the only enemy. Much more on this in the next book.

So if you do find yourself doing this, why not stop. Why not give up being a victim, stop replaying yourself created hurts and remember that no one ever causes your pain. It's only and always you. Am I repeating myself here? Is it getting to you that I'm repeating myself? Feeling a little irritated by all this repetition? Who is creating your irritation? Thank you!

Don't make the past a pest

Look how much time you spend in the past. See how often you visit yesterday. Watch how frequently you refer to what is stone dead and long gone. Observe how you live for the past in the present. Witness how, when you look into the future you are using the past as both the reference points and the raw material to create tomorrow. Oh sweet past, you were wonderful, but now you are gone. Fare thee well my past, goodbye to history. I am now fully present in the here and now. There is only now. I am now. I am. I.

The SIXTH Response to Hurt
Karming

So you want to take responsibility for your hurt by acknowledging it's payback time and you recognise you are being paid back

Yes, you are right, there is probably no such word as karming! If there were it would mean that you are *applying your understanding of 'karmic law' to make sense of what has happened to you,* and in so doing successfully transcending all of the five previous responses. The law of karma is simply the law of cause and effect or, in the specific context of human relationship, the law of reciprocity.

The concept of karma is simple. What you send out you get back. Each one of us is sending out all the time. Thoughts, feelings, attitudes and actions are the packages we radiate into the world of our relationships, every moment of every day. And it all comes back... eventually. This is the principle of karma at its simplest level – sowing and reaping, action and reaction, what goes around comes around.

Karma is the law of reciprocity and it's the iron-clad law of the universe. Understand and accept karma and you understand and accept that any hurt, that means any hurt, however severe, is always simply the return of previous thoughts/attitudes/actions in the past. A past that may only be moments ago. You give out positive and positive will come back. You give out negative and negative will return. In short the universal debt settler and collector will come to settle or collect.

For many people, this idea is too neat, too simple, too implausible. Is this so for you? All I can say is perhaps you have not yet explored this principle that makes the world go round at all levels, in all places, in all circumstances. It's not surprising that it's not widely understood, because it's just not part of our formal education. Perhaps you are just not ready to see and take responsibility for your feelings in particular, or your actions in general. Perhaps you intuitively know the consequences of what you think and do, and those consequences are too painful to acknowledge. Perhaps it's just a bridge too far to accept that every single little event is both an effect and a cause, a domino being felled, and then felling the next domino along the line. If you can see and accept the precision of this law of human motion, then when your head bumps the dashboard when you suddenly have to stop your car in traffic, you realise the resulting pain is the return of your karma. Somewhere in the past, you set the sequence of events in motion that now returns to cause the meeting of your head and the dashboard. See this, accept this, and you will never ever blame anyone for anything ever again. You will also become much more aware of the quality of your thoughts and much more discerning of the nature of your actions.

Or perhaps all this 'karma theory' just leaves you with more questions unanswered than answered. If so, send me the questions and let's talk. Perhaps you find yourself trapped in old habits of whinging, whining and complaining about others, about the weather, about life. It's one of your old records that you keep playing. Stop playing the record entitled 'life is bad' and start recording a new record called 'life is good, great, fantastic'. And so it will be. Start sending out that positive energy and that's exactly what you will begin to feel and, as a bonus, it's what you will attract back. You only have to mean it. It is that simple.

If you don't want to look so close to home for evidence of karmic patterns, simply watch the daily news and you will see karma playing itself out. The Palestinians and the Israelis, the British and the Irish, Rangers and Celtic, Coca Cola and Pepsi, Muslims and Christians. They are all false identities of course. That's where the karma begins. It starts in the creation of, and attachment to, a false identity of oneself. In reality there is no such thing as Irish, British, Muslim, Jew, etc. They are simply labels. But as long as humans are conditioned to identify with a label they will always see other labels as threats and act with fear, which will lead to violence and therefore karmic patterns which the two parties jointly conspire to co-create. The karma may occasionally die down, but it will continue to erupt and expand over time, until one party wakes up and realises they are asleep to the truth of who they really are, and begins to see the other not as a threat, but as someone who simply holds a different set of beliefs. And beliefs are not the truth.

That's the elementary lesson in karma. Here is the advanced lesson. Your karma is a record of all the actions you have ever done, and it is mostly held in your subconscious, outside your day-to-day awareness. At the deepest level that record includes your beliefs. If you have learned to believe that the words and actions of others can affect your feelings, then you will create your karma (your record of action) accordingly. You will create traits and habits of reactiveness within your personality. You will create yourself as a reactive person. You will send visible and invisible packets of energy at others whom you believe have caused you to feel hurt. Those packets will not contain positive energy, and it will not be long before they come back. But that's a secondary issue.

Before you send those nasty little packets, you first create them and then you feel them yourself, and as a consequence you are in effect hurting yourself with your own creation. It's not long before it becomes a habit, then a permanent fixture within your personality. Now that's really daft, is it not? In other words, when you get angry at someone, who suffers first and most? That's instant karma. Then, every time you see the person that you wrongly think caused your hurt, you will repeat the record of your anger and suffer again, thereby strengthening the illusion that it is them, and not you, who is responsible for your unhappiness. If you sustain the pattern of this reaction, your karma will not only expand and 'ripple' into your relationships, it will eventually 'cripple' your conscious ability to stay calm, at peace, coherent and positive whenever you communicate with that person. Over time, that will expand into your communication with anyone who reminds you of that person. Over time, it will cripple your ability to communicate with everyone. Unless you resolve your karma, unless you dispel the illusion upon which the original action was based, which is to realise and accept that it was not them that caused your suffering (your anger) in the first place, you will be a mental and emotional cripple for life.

Let's take another example. Let's say you worry a lot. You have created a record, a pattern of worry at a mental and emotional level. Not long after you 'lay down' this record within your consciousness, within yourself, it starts to 'play you'. It becomes a habit. You will even identify with it and sometimes say, "I am such a worrier." You will probably even justify your worry with the commonly held belief that it's good to worry. You may even think to yourself, "I am a good worrier because it demonstrates that I care!" Which of course is complete nonsense, because worry is fear and care is love, and they are polar opposites.

But let's follow through and see where this leads. Your 'worry karma' is now recorded and fixed in your consciousness. It is triggered by anything in life that triggers a negative memory of the past. Worry is really a negatively perceived past, repackaged and projected into the future. It means, once again, you are suffering, and you are probably under the illusion that you are enjoying your suffering, especially when you form a 'worry club' with friends over morning coffee. It also means you are not living now. You are missing your own life by living in your worries, which are always in the past and in the future. Your worry habit has trapped you in the past where you get the raw material for your worries, and a non-existent future, where you project that material, and the result is you miss your life now. All this won't change until you choose to change the worry habits that you have recorded in your consciousness. That will require the dissolving of the illusion that it's good and necessary to worry, with the truth that worrying about anything is simply 'fantisised catastrophising'. It's a waste of time and energy. It means replacing the urge to create images of catastrophic futures with positive responses to what is happening in your life right now. Otherwise your 'worry karma' will have you in permanent pain.

A Note to the Sceptical

If you don't believe in the law of reciprocity, look for evidence in your own life. When someone does you a favour, watch how you are moved to do the same for that person or for someone else. If you walk into the office and smile at everyone, watch how they smile back, however reluctantly. And those who don't at first will eventually, if you sustain your smile strategy – it's as if they have to. Give money to charity and watch how it returns from the most unlikely places. It's all about energy and its flow, its movement, its rippling, its reflecting. Why? Because everything is energy. Karma is action, and action is energy at work! At every level. Simple really!

The SEVENTH Response to Hurt
Enlightening

So you want to see, know and live the absolute truth about hurt and forgiveness

Are you sitting comfortably? It's likely you are either going to love this, hate this or simply not understand this. Take a moment to make your mind very peaceful. Remember that peace is your nature and you are at your most powerful and most receptive when you are in your 'natural state'. Then slowly read the following.

No one ever, ever, ever hurts you ... ever. It's always you who hurts yourself... or seems to! Ultimately you cannot even hurt yourself, you can only disturb an illusion that you wrongly think is you.

To see the truth of this, you will need to be aware of what you are doing within your consciousness. In order to see and understand this absolute truth, you will need to recognise who and what you truly are – spirit not form, soul not body. Only then can you cease to be upset when people criticise (attack) your physical shape, features, dress or personality. Only then will you be able to realise that while your body may be jabbed, punched or stabbed the pain you feel is only a signal from your body, and because you are not your body you can choose not to the feel the pain. Not an easy choice to make, but it can be made. (I'm not recommending you deliberately go looking for ways to test or prove this.)

To see the truth, you will also need to stop identifying with your thoughts and feelings, with your beliefs and perceptions. They are not you; they are just your creation.

So let's back up a bit here and get really clear about what's being said.

There are two kinds of hurt, physical hurt and non-physical hurt. Let's do physical hurt first.

Physical hurt

We have all heard of the pain barrier. Athletes run through it when they train and perform in endurance events. In fact, all kinds of people know how to do this. You can go to the doctors in some parts of the world and they will perform serious operations, even amputations, without anaesthetic and you won't feel a thing. All you have to do is put your tongue to the roof of your mouth! Acupuncturists can divert pain sensations away from your brain. You even do it semi-consciously when you become so absorbed by what's on TV that you lose all sense of your toothache. All this goes to show, but not prove (you have to do that for yourself), that there is your body with its five senses that creates signals to the brain, then there is you, the operator of the brain, and therefore the boss. So with a little training, it is possible to go beyond the sensation of physical pain. It is possible not to register any physical discomfort whatsoever. The key word here is training. Going beyond physical pain is another of those things we never learn to do. Yogis, athletes and the David Blaines of this world do learn, and they do it in public, some more successfully than others. The point here is that, while it is important to feel the pain, you don't have to sustain the feeling. You can learn to go beyond it. But first it is vital to acknowledge it and respond to the message it represents in the right way. That can range from a band-aid to medical treatment.

The habit we mostly develop is to sustain the pain and identify with pain. You replay in your mind the images of the situation that seemed to cause your pain. You attribute the pain to the rock that bumped into your foot, or the knife in the other person's hand, which you happened to walk into! The bottom line is that rocks and knives did not hurt YOU, they hurt your body, they scratched the corporeal form which you animate and inhabit, but they cannot touch YOU.

So let's say someone does enter a knife into your body or lands a brick on your head. What do you do? How are you to deal with this so that you are not left blaming, resenting and even hating the person who did it? Two ways forward here. First you can use the 'stuff happens' philosophy, as many people do, heal the physical wounds with the right treatment, drop the memory of the event, and move on.

Not easy if you've lost limbs or your senses are impaired. The alternative? To continue adding emotional pain to your physical pain, long after the actual event.

The second strategy is a little deeper. It starts with realising there are no accidents or random events in life. Everything has a cause and a reason. Whatever happened, happened for a reason. Perhaps it happened to shake you out of a comfortable autopilot life. Perhaps because there is a lesson you need to learn. Perhaps you needed to be tested. And then there is the cause. Many people intuitively realise karmic patterns in their life and fully recognise that whatever comes to them has been set in motion some time, somewhere within their actions in the past. This understanding, as we have already seen, allows you to take responsibility for your experience, which in effect means to be the master of the situation, not create anger and resentment, not see and identify yourself as a victim, and get on with your life. You could even say that the universal debt collector just called and you were able to settle an outstanding debt. Some of the burden of your past karmas has been relieved.

Mental and emotional hurt

So let's do the other kind of hurt or suffering that 'seems' to have been caused by others, but wasn't, i.e. mental and emotional hurt (that's if you are still reading and you haven't thrown this book out the window).

There are first-person hurts, which 'appear' to have been inflicted directly upon you personally. Then there are second-person hurts, where you feel hurt because someone else seems to have been hurt, and you identify with their pain. You may even hear yourself say, "I feel your pain" in order to try to make the other person feel better. In the light of truth the first is ridiculous, and the second is almost laughable, if it were not for the fact that so many of us are so fast asleep under the illusion that it's only right to suffer when others suffer.

First-person hurts

Let's say you call me stupid, you insult my work, you criticise my actions, you question my motives, you call me a liar, you blame me for something I have not done. Of course you may think I am going to feel hurt. You might even say it is natural that I feel hurt. You probably designed your words in order to hurt me. The world would condone my angry defensiveness as justified. But wait a minute. I have a choice. I can choose not to feel hurt by your words, by your attitude. I can choose not to react. I can choose to say, "You may perceive me as stupid, but I don't perceive me as stupid." I can choose to say, "Yes, that may have been a silly thing to have done or said, but it doesn't make me a stupid person." I could say, "You may call me a liar or question my motives, but I know I'm not a liar and that I meant well." It takes power and presence of mind to make these choices. It may take a little practice. But it is possible. We all know someone who seems to never get hurt, never reacts, and to whom all such comments are like water off the proverbial duck's back. It demonstrates that it is possible. When you do make this choice, it also proves that it's never the other person who creates your hurt, it is always you. Now expand this truth out a little wider and it means that no one actually hurts anyone else ever. Therefore there is no need for forgiveness. Mmm ... not convinced are you?

Let's do it again, but this time I am going to say these nasty little lines to you. I want you to be aware of what you are doing with them in your head. I call you stupid. And you feel hurt. Why? Because you are carrying an image of yourself as being a 'not stupid person' in your mind. In fact you are attached to that image of yourself to the extent it has become your identity. So now my judgment, in the form of words comes flying at you and you take it into your consciousness, and because it contradicts the image you have of yourself, to which you are attached and identified, you become emotionally disturbed. You start to defend yourself, your image of yourself, against a perceived threat that you see in my words. The first line of your defence is your anger. This is called ego. You are in pain, not because of the 'word symbols' I threw at you, but because of what you do with them in your mind. If you were not attached to the image of being Mr or Ms Always Very Bright and Clever, then being called stupid would not bother you. You might just disagree. In fact you would respond from the sound self knowledge that yes, sometimes you do things which are not so sensible, but that you are not a stupid person. Outcome? No mental disturbance, no pain, no hurt.

One of the secrets here is to remind yourself that you are not your personality, you are not your actions, your words or even your thoughts. They are your creation, but they are not you. You are the creator. So when someone judges and denigrates any of those things that you create, you don't take it personally. If you do take it personally, it means that you will have hurt yourself because of your attachment to and identification with the things (thoughts, feelings, personality). It is your attachment that is the cause of your pain. When you see this and accept this, then truly you will realise you are the creator of ALL your own hurt... always, no matter what the situation or event. Then the only person that you need to forgive is yourself. Always and only yourself. Why? Because you simply fell asleep to the true you, the real you. The imperishable, untouchable and unhurtable you.

Quite challenging, isn't it? Why? Because we have all been conditioned to believe the opposite. It's why we watch the soaps and go to the movies. It's why some of us are always spoiling for an argument or a fight. So we can blame someone else for what we feel and justify the projection of our pain on to them.

So the truth is out. It's always and only you. But even that is an illusion. If you are still holding this book in your hand, it might be a good idea to reread, contemplate, meditate, cogitate on the last few paragraphs. I guarantee that when the penny drops, your life will change forever. Such is the power of truth. Once you 'get it' all you have to do is practise it in real life. But we haven't finished yet. One more level to go.

The grandest illusion of all

Another way to say this, or see this, is to realise that you weren't hurt, but your ego was disturbed. Your 'essential self' was not hurt, but your ego was the cause of the discomfort. As we have already seen (did you see it?), ego is when you create an image on the screen of your mind (you are not your mind, but you have a mind) and then YOU get attached to that image, to such an extent that you lose your sense of self in the image. It becomes your identity. When someone attacks that image , it seems and feels like they are attacking you. They may even think they are attacking you. But they are not. They are attacking an illusion. For you are not an image on your mind, you are you. The untouchable and undisturbable you, that is a source of constant peace, love and joy. But when you lose connection, lose awareness of who you really are, and you identify with an image that you have created in your mind, then anything that challenges that image will be taken personally. Peace, love and joy disappear instantly and you feel an inner disturbance of your mind, called emotion! Emotion simply means agitation of mind, and because you are identifying with what's on your mind, you 'feel' that agitation, and you think it's happening to you because of what 'they' said/did.

Actually, the person who is mounting the attack, judgement or insult towards you is also acting from their pain. They have an image of how they would like you to be or do. They are attached to that image and identify with it, and when you do not act or be according to that image, they make themselves upset and hurt. But they believe that you have made them feel that way. So they attack you as a kind of revenge. In effect, they are attacking a double illusion. Simple isn't it? Well, it's complicated until you simplify it. And only you can do that for you.

Another way to say it is that you only hurt yourself when you try to hurt another. Then it's a double hurt because, while you are doing it, deep down, at the very heart of your consciousness, where you innately and always know the truth, it's as if you subconsciously know you are acting against the truth that you are untouchable and unhurtable. That's why, after an emotional outburst at someone, when you calm down, there is usually a little voice of regret. This is the voice of your conscience, which is trying to let you know you just acted against what is true. You just went against the grain, so to speak. So you then hurt yourself for making a mistake. Subtle, isn't it? This is why, as soon as you realise that you have made a mistake by acting against the truth, it becomes quite important to forgive yourself fast and not continue to blame yourself for making a mistake. The mistake after all, is just to forget who and what you are, for a moment, and then act out of that ignorance.

So ultimately no one ever hurts anyone else and we only hurt ourselves, but not our real self, which can never be hurt, no matter what. We only disturb what is our false sense of self, the ego. It is the false sense of self that is disturbable, but our true self is undisturbable.

Easy isn't.it? Questions? I am sure you have many. I am almost certain all the above is not clear, perhaps it is even 'disturbing', especially if you are encountering such ideas for the first time. Try not to fight it, pooh-pooh it out of hand, but look, reflect and contemplate the ideas. Pose a specific question based on a real life situation and then see if you can answer the question yourself, using the insights above.

Hey, it's been great talking to you. You probably guessed that I tend to write as I talk. Hope you managed to follow my trains of thought, and you found the style conducive to your growing understanding. I also hope to see you some day in the flesh, perhaps at a seminar or a retreat. Then you can give me a hard time on all of these fascinating aspects of the journey we all now share, the journey home. You do realise you are on your way home, don't you? Where home, for all who wander in the jungle of illusion, is simply the truth.

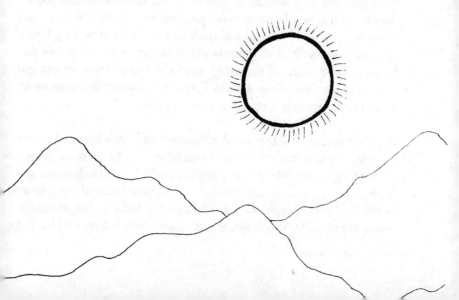

The Enlightened Apology

So there you have it. No one ever makes you angry... ever! True or false? If it is now true for you, then the other way round must also be true. Which means you can never make anyone else angry. You can never make another suffer. If you follow the trail of insights throughout this book, it is the logical conclusion. However, to truly arrive at that conclusion, with conviction, you will need to see it from the highest spiritual point of view (see page 11). As we have seen, this is not an easy level of awareness to reach in day-to-day reality, much of which is really unreality! You will need to go beyond psychological understanding and into spiritual truth, to both see and be beyond the illusion that something outside YOU has the power to affect you. Hence the need for the regular practice of meditation.

Let's play with the ramifications of this one insight one more time! Let's say that you start to think, "Mmm... great, now I can say and do what I like to others, and if that's a problem for them, then that's their problem not mine." This thought is the doorway to arrogance and a miserable life. If you do decide to live according to this philosophy, it won't be long before others send you lots of negative energy. It won't be long before others avoid you and even isolate you. But more importantly, more insightfully, it means that although you may have realised that you are responsible for all your feelings, you may not have fully realised that if you violate this law, i.e. create any form of violent or negative energy, from your intention through to your behaviour towards another, you are the one who suffers first and most, each and every time you do it. You shoot yourself in the mental and spiritual foot. It won't be long before you can hardly walk at all in the world of human relationship. Not just because of the nature of the energy that others may return to you, but because of what you do to yourself. Your karma (action) will generate an instant return entirely within your consciousness.

If the ultimate truth is that you don't actually ever cause hurt and sorrow for others, would that mean you would never have to say sorry or even ask for forgiveness? Well yes, and no! You could follow the letter of that truth, so to speak, and never apologise to anyone for anything you say or do. And some people do. But that's usually because they are totally insensitive to the feelings of others or they genuinely have not yet learned how to care for others or they are just too fearful to admit they may have done something wrong. And that means they are still asleep in their own ignorance, and therefore still suffering themselves.

When someone suffers after you speak or act, it's not so much a question of do I apologise or not, but more a question of 'levels of enlightenment'. If you know the other person still believes that their hurt is caused by someone other than themselves, and if you inadvertently say or do something to which they become upset, then saying sorry is entirely appropriate, and the way to keep the relationship intact. However, be careful of two things. First, that by saying sorry you don't then encourage them to react to any little thing you say or do. If they sense that you are affected by their reaction then they may start to react so that you react. The saying 'it's the squeaky hinge that gets the oil' springs to mind here. Even the most mature, responsible and sensible people can fall into this old pattern. The second 'be careful' is that if you do say 'sorry' make sure that you don't actually create real sorrow within yourself. If you do then all you do is disempower yourself. Saying 'sorry' in such instances really means, "I realise that you have not yet realised that your suffering is your creation, not mine". You can't say this of course. It would probably sound condescending, and the other person would likely wonder which planet you were visiting from!

If you know the other is enlightened in this area of self-responsibility, and they still occasionally react and blame others, including yourself, for their upset, saying sorry is ridiculous for both parties. Better to say something like, "Are you aware you are playing victim and projecting yourself created pain again?" You would, of course, find your own way to say it. In so doing you serve to awaken the other from a sleepy moment where they fell back under the spell of the old illusion that 'others make me feel'. And if you are good friends then you would hope they would do the same for you, should you occasionally fall asleep yourself.

To think, "Why should I say sorry, I'm enlightened about these things," is the arrogance of ego, which means you are really still asleep. But to actually be in a real state of sorrow yourself, when you say sorry, is to attempt to hurt yourself. That's ego again. Keep doing that (which is what some people do) and it will turn into anger at yourself, and eventually guilt, and eventually you will start to judge and criticise others as you project your anger to avoid your guilt. And so this inner vicious cycle continues.

The most enlightened apology is towards yourself, when you realise that you only ever attempt to hurt yourself. This self-hurt has become a habit over time, it is a learned tendency, threaded through your character. If you continue to make this mistake, then as soon as you become aware of it, say sorry to yourself, forgive yourself, have mercy on yourself, remind yourself of the truth and move on. As this habit of emotional self-harm atrophies, you will begin to find and feel your true peaceful, loving nature as it emerges from your spiritual heart, once hardened by self-created suffering, which has now been softened and healed by the restoration of truth.

And finally there is the apologiser who is always seeking the forgiveness of others. Here the road forks again. Down one path is genuine contrition for saying or doing something against the grain of the law of love, where love means union or connection. As we saw earlier, to judge, criticise, attempt to control or blame others are all forms of 'love breaking' acts, which create separation. As soon as you become aware of what you are doing, simply forgive yourself by correcting your mistake and remind yourself that love is your true nature and the true nature of all others. If the other person is upset, it means that they too are acting against the law of love. They are making a similar mistake. They have disconnected from the truth within themselves that says no one else is responsible for what I think and feel AND love is what I am. They may say they forgive, but they are unlikely to forget, which means they have not really forgiven. However, they are unlikely to be aware of that.

Down the other path is the apologiser who has learned that love can only be felt when they get the attention, acceptance and approval of others. They are compulsive needers and seekers. They may consciously or subconsciously speak and act in ways they know will elicit attention. They are often drawn to people they know who are easily offended or affected by small things. Their mantra in life becomes, "Sorry!", which decoded really means, "Here I am please acknowledge me, attend to me and accept me", which decoded really means, "Please give me your love." This neediness can ~~only~~ be cured when they do some spiritual work and realise they already have within them what they consciously or unconsciously seek from others.

In summary, say 'sorry' only until the other realises that they create their own sorrow. Never create sorrow in yourself when you say sorry. Challenge others to awaken to the truth of their self-responsibility, according to how ready you think they are to awaken. There is no need to seek the forgiveness of others if you know that they know that they only hurt themselves. You can only ever forgive yourself. The deepest level of forgiveness is the realisation of the truth that YOU cannot be hurt. The truth is that which never changes. And the truth is you are peace, you are love and, while you lose awareness of that truth, nothing can ever damage that truth. It is only possible to be truly nourished by love when you don't need love from others. Only then are you able to receive it!

In a Nutshell

Anger

A self-created disturbance of the energy of your consciousness when
any desire is not fulfilled, when you believe you have been hurt by
another or when you believe you have lost
something which was never yours, which
is everything that is not you.

Peace

The core state of you, the spiritual being. That which can never
be lost or taken from you, but which you lose awareness of.
It is the very ground of your being
and it is also your power.

Forgiveness

What you may believe you have to do when you believe someone has
hurt you, or what you might want others to give you when you believe
you have hurt them. It is an act of the love that you are,
which ultimately does not need to act in this way
when the truth that no one can hurt YOU,
no one can touch YOU, is restored
to your awareness.

In truth the only 'real' forgiveness is the realisation that
love is what you are and love can never be hurt. Love is
forgiving, which means 'for giving'. When you forget
this truth your life becomes time spent 'for getting'.
That's when the illusion of hurt is born.

Peace is – Love does – Truth guides – Happiness rewards

Thanks and Links

Thanks to all at the Global Retreat Centre for the
silent space to 'see' in the most powerful place to 'be'
www.globalretreatcentre.com

Thanks to Reed Learning for the oportunity to 'pass on'
www.reed.co.uk/learning

Thanks to Bliss for the kind of music which relaxes
heart and soul, and induces the occasional AHA!
www.blissfulmusic.com

Thanks to Marneta for showing us all how to
reach the hearts of the children of the world
www.relaxkids.com

Thanks to the Brahma Kumaris World Spiritual
University where anyone can receive free tuition
in meditation in thousands of centres across
90 countries
www.bkwsu.org

Thanks and buckets of love to my sisters and
brothers for your ever present subtle support

For more insights, workshops, retreats, seminars,
talks, articles and meditations please see:
www.relax7.com
www.SpiritualIntelligenceUnit.com
www.awarenessretreats.com
www.learn-meditation.com

About the Author

Based in the Cotswolds and London, Mike George is a best-selling author, spiritual teacher and management tutor.

In a unique blend of insight, wisdom and humour, Mike brings together the three key strands of 21st century – emotional/spiritual intelligence, management/leadership development and continuous learning. His retreat-style leadership courses in the Cotswolds, and one-day intensive courses in London, run monthly and include; Liberating Leadership; The Missing Link in Management Development; Spiritual Intelligence at Work; Emotional Intelligence; and Conflict Resolution.

As a teacher of meditation and spiritual development for over 20 years, Mike guides and coaches individuals, executives and small management groups in over 30 countries in the art and practice of meditation.

He is the founder of The Relaxation Centre (*www.relax7.com*) and Director of the Spiritual Intelligence Unit (*www.SpiritualIntelligenceUnit.com*). Each year he leads regular awareness and enlightenment retreats across the world including Africa, Australia, Argentina, Brazil, Chile, Croatia, Germany, Italy, Mexico, Scandinavia, Spain and throughout the UK and USA (*www.awarenessretreats.com*)

Now in 15 languages, his other publications include; *The 7 AHAs of Highly Enlightened Souls; The Secrets of Self Management; Learn to Relax; Learn to Find Inner Peace; In the Light of Meditation – A Guide to Spiritual Development; 1001 Meditations.*

Mike can be contacted at *mike@relax7.com* and a schedule of his seminars and talks can be found at *www.relax7.com/diary*

If you would like to subscribe (free) to Mikes *Clear Thinking* weekly email please send your request to mike@relax7.com